Practical Strategies to Assess Value in Health Care

Craig A. Solid

Practical Strategies to Assess Value in Health Care

 Springer

Craig A. Solid
Owner and Principal
Solid Research Group, LLC
SAINT PAUL, MN, USA

ISBN 978-3-030-95151-1   ISBN 978-3-030-95149-8   (eBook)
https://doi.org/10.1007/978-3-030-95149-8

This Springer imprint is published by the registered company Springer Nature Switzerland AG
The registered company address is: Gewerbestrasse 11, 6330 Cham, Switzerland

To my family, for all that you do, Emily, Vieva, Emmett, and Kipp.

Preface

I have been deeply entrenched in the assessment and analysis of various components of health care for over 20 years. From the late 1990s to today, I have witnessed first-hand the shift toward "value-based" care in policy and reimbursement, but also in how individuals and organizations have come to view their role in the vast and complex machinery we know as the healthcare industry. Through my work with clients and personal research, I have come to notice significant gaps in the resources available to healthcare professionals who seek to assess value, financial or otherwise. This is lamentable, given that the great majority of healthcare professionals are motivated, hardworking individuals who are passionate about improving the quality and value of health care.

Almost without exception, the individuals I have encountered in this industry are committed to their own improvement and open to learning new skills, so that they may be better equipped to tackle the many challenges faced when attempting to change care delivery systems. Unfortunately, there exists a paucity of information or guidance when needing to plan, execute, and summarize assessments of the value of an intervention, product, device, or process.

I wrote my previous book, *Return on Investment for Healthcare Quality Improvement*, for healthcare professionals needing to quantify the financial return of particular decisions or quality initiatives. The book compiles the ideas and techniques I have used to help clients secure funding or justify particular activities and provides a general structure that can be applied to a variety of situations, settings, and motivations. The feedback I have received suggests that it was successful in beginning to fill some of the gaps in value-related resources available to healthcare professionals.

However, I came to confirm through subsequent conversations with individuals across the spectrum of care (some of whom had read the book, some who had not) that there remained a sizable gap surrounding the assessment of value more generally. Discussions with clinicians, patient advocates, administrators, policy makers, and private business owners revealed a universal craving for more specifics regarding definitions and interpretations of value. Given the increasingly important role value plays across the landscape of health care in the USA, a shared understanding of how to think and talk about value has never been more critical. Yet, the variety of perspectives (patients, providers, clinicians, policy makers, etc.) from which to view value and the myriad of motivations to assess value make it impossible to establish a single, universally applicable definition of value. Instead, we need to learn how to *think about* value, so that when faced with a specific situation or decision, we can develop an appropriate definition and identify the relevant benefits, costs, and metrics for our unique circumstances.

This book presents a framework to help guide the development and execution of informative value assessments. Through examinations of concepts and theories from network science, economics, and behavioral science, I present key components to consider and address as one establishes an appropriate value definition and the elements needed to quantify and describe it. Using a common framework can homogenize how assessments are performed and as a result make them more comparable. As with my previous book, the tools and ideas presented in the following pages were born from my work with clients. I have used these techniques to help clients determine and demonstrate value, which in turn has helped them make a business case for their intervention, device, or product to funders, investors, customers, or organizations they want to partner with or be acquired by.

I wrote this book with a variety of healthcare professionals in mind. Clinicians, quality improvement implementers, facility administrators, board members, policy makers, device manufacturers, med-tech/digital health companies, investors, and others will all find relevant concepts and techniques that will enhance their ability to assess, discuss, and recognize value. While the financial implications of increasing revenues or decreasing costs are essential to the viability of healthcare infrastructure and care delivery systems, the value of health care includes nonmonetary benefits like quality of life, patient experiences, mental and emotional well-being, security, equity, hope, and innumerable other things. Therefore, the scope of this book is as broad as possible, encompassing all types of value one could imagine. It is my sincere hope that in the pages that follow you will find insight and inspiration for your own value assessments.

I am appreciative to the many individuals and organizations who have allowed me to assist them with their value-related needs and have been willing to engage in conversations about value. I would like to explicitly acknowledge a few individuals, including Andrew Kopolow, Becca Etz, Laurie Knutson, John Nelson, and Adan Becerra, for their thoughts and insights regarding the topic of value. I owe a particular debt to Rebecca Smith for her careful reading and insightful feedback on a preliminary draft of this book. And of course, I would be remiss if I did not acknowledge my wife, Emily, for her unwavering support and confidence in this and all endeavors.

Saint Paul, MN, USA   Craig A. Solid

Contents

About the Author

Craig A. Solid, PhD is an independent consultant who is the owner and principal of Solid Research Group, LLC. He helps a variety of organizations, including device and digital health companies, demonstrate and communicate the value of their product, device, process, or solution. He has more than 22 years of experience in health care and has co-authored over 60 peer-reviewed manuscripts and multiple books. He regularly gives seminars and guest lectures on value in health care and value assessments. His most recent book, *Return on Investment for Healthcare Quality Improvement,* is available from Springer (2020). Dr. Solid lives in St. Paul, Minnesota, with his wife and three children.

Abbreviations

ACA	Affordable Care Act
ACO	Accountable care organization
BCR	Benefit-to-cost ratio
CAS	Complex adaptive system
CBO	Community-based organizations
CEA	Cost-effectiveness analysis
CLABSI	Central line-associated bloodstream infection
CMS	Centers for Medicare & Medicaid Services
CUA	Cost–utility analysis
ED	Emergency department
EHR	Electronic health record
FFS	Fee-for-service
ICER	Incremental cost-effectiveness ratio
MACRA	Medicare Access and CHIP Reauthorization Act
QALY	Quality-adjusted life year
RCT	Randomized controlled trial
ROI	Return on investment
TPHO	Third-party healthcare organization

Chapter 1
Introduction

1.1 Value in Health Care

1.1.1 Value as a Concept

These days, the idea of value is at the center of many activities and decisions within the US healthcare system. At the most micro level, individual hospitals and clinics decide on investments in infrastructure, equipment, and quality improvement activities based, in part, on the increase in value they are likely to realize. At the macro level, national policy makers construct quality monitoring programs that are linked to reimbursement mechanisms in an attempt to incentivize value-based care. In between, funders determine which programs or organizations to allocate money to and venture capitalists choose which device or med-tech company to support, all with the intent to increase value, but for whom? Many of these decisions about what to invest in are simply the business of health care—improving financial outcomes for providers and payers—while other investment decisions more directly strive to improve value from the patient perspective. Community-based organizations (CBOs), nonprofits, doctors, nurses, advocates, caregivers, and many others also actively seek solutions that will improve the value that patients get from the care they receive.

Some books detail the technical steps for carrying out a specific type of value assessment, such as cost-effectiveness analysis or return on investment, but a paucity of resources attempt to teach healthcare professionals how to *think* about value. This is unfortunate because as we move forward in our collective journey to increase the value of care, all healthcare professionals should be well versed in the language and concepts of value, its components, and its implications. Every healthcare professional affects the value of care, so it would be beneficial for every healthcare professional to understand value.

© The Author(s), under exclusive license to Springer Nature Switzerland AG 2022
C. A. Solid, *Practical Strategies to Assess Value in Health Care*,
https://doi.org/10.1007/978-3-030-95149-8_1

Understanding how to consider, approach, plan, conduct, and communicate a value assessment requires an exploration of the constructs and assumptions upon which our various definitions of value depend. Those seeking to actively assess value will struggle to produce an effective, informative assessment without first considering the underlying framework used when applying a specific method, technique, or analysis. When we do not understand the underlying and/or use an inappropriate framework, the results of a value assessment will fail to provide the insight required by those who look to leverage the information for decision-making. If this seems hyperbolic, consider a 2019 systematic review [1] of methods used to assess value, where the authors identified "22 distinct approaches to assess the value of health care interventions" among the 38 articles they reviewed. They concluded that the most common method among them (cost-effectiveness analysis) "has not been sufficient to meet the needs of decision-makers." This notion that the most common tools used to assess value in the healthcare industry are insufficient to meet the needs of decision makers indicates that there is a breakdown in the most fundamental axioms of how we think about value in health care.

Clearly, we need to shift our thinking. We in health care are too heavily invested (mentally, emotionally, and financially) in the aspirational goal of promoting and supporting value in health care to not demand a more comprehensive and universal approach for assessing value that is relevant for anyone who claims to have an interest in improving care and patient outcomes. Current policy, opinions, research, and the strategies of for-profit payers all point to a future where care is chosen, delivered, and paid for within a value-based framework. Yet, as an industry we have no shared vernacular for how to talk about value; our opinions differ on how value should be defined, measured, quantified, and compared. And, as indicated by the review mentioned previously, our current methods are insufficient to meet our needs to help us decide where to place our efforts and our resources.

I propose that we invest some time and resources into collectively examining the concept of value, including how it is described, defined, measured, and compared. Additionally, I do not believe that one universal construct or method is applicable across situations or topic areas. Instead, I believe that helping healthcare professionals learn how to think about value is a better path forward. When equipped with the knowledge necessary to think critically about a situation and its interrelated components, these healthcare professionals can then determine how best to assess value in a given situation or for a specific purpose. With a deep understanding of what comprises value in any given situation and being well versed in a variety of tools to measure it, they can tailor a value assessment to meet their unique needs and inform specific decisions knowing that others will be able to understand what was done and why. If a shared understanding of how to think about value is fostered, people will have a shared language to discuss, debate, and build on one another's efforts. With this shared understanding and language, the practice of assessing and describing value can evolve and grow as needs change and information is gathered.

It should be noted that establishing a concrete definition of value should not necessarily be the goal. Like quality, "value" is subjective and can differ based on circumstances and point of view. But like the definitions of quality that are now commonly used, any definition and representation of value should have certain characteristics that remain constant across definitions. As stated by the authors of the review article described previously, "…we do not expect that there is only one correct 'value' for any intervention, even for a specific condition, i.e., 'value' is contextual." Clearly, then, we need a functional framework for how to think about value that is adaptable and applicable across settings, conditions, and activities.

If we are going to link payment of and investments into the healthcare system to an idea of value, we should be clear about what that idea is. The hope, then, is that through a deep exploration into the nature of health, health care, economics, quality, innovation, and human factors we can begin to establish some basic tenets for what should always be considered when we speak of value, and more practically, to develop a framework for developing and performing a value assessment.

In this text, we will explore the notion of value in health care in an attempt to better understand what it means, as well as how to measure and compare it. We will:

- Consider relevant perspectives (e.g., patients, payers, providers, policy makers, and society) and audiences.
- Explore different motivations and desired outcomes for measuring and sharing information about value.
- Discuss pertinent economic concepts that can influence value or the perception of value (e.g., moral hazard, price insensitivity, etc.).
- Ponder theories from the field of network science to describe how healthcare delivery systems and the individuals within those systems behave and make decisions.
- Define possible metrics for measuring value and explore related methods.
- Consider human factors that give meaning to value measurements.
- Analyze practical constraints to measuring value.
- Develop a structure for how to think about, design, and carry out value assessments.

1.1.1.1 Value: What It Is and What It Isn't

Initially, value-based care was championed by policy makers and invoked through the Affordable Care Act and the Medicare Access and CHIP Reauthorization Act (MACRA) of 2015; they did this by linking reimbursement to performance on quality measures. MACRA, specifically, mandated the creation of an incentive program where provider reimbursement would partially depend on providers' performance on quality metrics. This practice is rooted in the notion that value can be summarized as "quality per dollar spent," which has been a common rallying cry among certain crowds within the healthcare industry. This oversimplification unfortunately defines one subjective notion (value) by using another (quality) and operates under the premise that the offering of financial carrots and sticks can incentivize clinicians and administrators to improve care quality.

In many academic papers, value is typically seen as a function of just two things: patient outcomes and costs, which is similar—and often identical—to the definition mentioned just previously of quality divided by cost. The definition of value as a function of patient outcomes and costs assumes that if you can improve outcomes and/or reduce costs, the value will automatically go up. Regardless of the intuitive appeal of this model for simple examples (e.g., improving outcomes while holding costs constant has value), this relationship ignores the inherent complexity that exists in healthcare delivery and the multiple perspectives (payers, providers, patients, other healthcare companies, caregivers, society, etc.) that are in play in any given situation. To see the flaw in this oversimplified model, one needs only to recognize that positive value from one perspective can be negative from another (e.g., fewer costs are good for payers and patients but represent less revenue for hospitals and clinics). It also lumps components of population health and care delivery into a single mechanism driving outcomes when we know that each plays a varying role in determining the fate of patients. Additionally, this model requires numerous assumptions about the validity and reliability of the chosen metric as a surrogate for quality as well as the attribution of that quality to patient outcomes.

While models like this can be useful and are often better than nothing at all, in some situations and circumstances a more robust framework for assessing value would likely lead to more accurate, relevant, and meaningful insight for making decisions or evaluating progress. Regardless of the situation, value varies by perspective, which means we need to examine all the relevant perspectives from which we might consider value. Stated more plainly, you cannot define value without answering the question: "Value to whom?" You cannot develop a universal definition of value that applies to all perspectives and situations simultaneously. In addition to specifying the perspective, definitions of value will almost always involve costs, benefits, and the relationship between them (e.g., their difference, their ratio, etc.). The relevant form of those components will depend on a number of factors, as we will soon see.

1.1.2 Value Perspectives

Throughout this book, we will consider the different perspectives that may be relevant to a particular value assessment. Because these terms may have different meanings in other texts, they are defined here for clarity.

Payers: In this text, these are insurance companies (both public and private) or purchasers of medical care who may fund initiatives intended to improve quality or lower costs in pursuit of higher profits.

Providers: These include anyone and everyone involved in care delivery. While the term likely prompts us to think of physicians or nurses, it also represents people involved in the business of providing care, like administrators, support staff, health IT, facility management, and so on. It is worth noting here when it may be appropriate to distinguish clinicians from those involved in the business of providing care.

When clinicians are included in this category it is in part because the provider perspective encompasses anything and everything involved in the delivery of care, and that is subject to the rules, regulations, and budgetary constraints involved in care delivery. However, in some distinct situations, the clinician perspective is separate (although perhaps complementary) to that of a facility administrator or others with whom they often share a perspective.

Patients: These include anyone who receives care. Sometimes, we will discuss family members or informal caregivers as having a separate perspective, but their perspectives are often linked or even the same as those of the patients.

Third-Party Healthcare Organizations (TPHOs): These include companies that create products, devices, systems, technology, or other solutions that providers use to care for patients. These include medical device companies that make pacemakers, prosthetics, or surgical tools; software and IT companies that make and support computer systems and electronic health records (EHRs); pharmaceutical companies; digital health/medical technology companies that facilitate care and diagnosis through digital innovations, and others. We can also think of CBOs as being part of this group, although at times it can be instructive to think of them as a separate perspective. This is because CBOs are often mission based, meaning that their incentives are aligned with patients or society and are not financially incentivized in the way that, say, device companies are. CBOs are groups that provide support services for those released from inpatient care or who are self-managing a chronic condition. Some provide mental or behavioral health services, some provide peer support, while others address social determinants of health such as access to transportation, Wi-Fi, and the like.

Society: This group is the most difficult to define because several components of societal value potentially stem from both population health and care delivery. Economists will talk about societal costs in terms of social burden, increases or decreases in the use of social services, losses to work productivity associated with absenteeism and effectiveness at work, leisure time, gross domestic product (GDP), and so on. In some senses, it is difficult to talk about the societal perspective because we may think of it as the "overall value to everyone"; but that notion is contrary to the idea we have already stated, namely that value is not the same for everyone and is dependent on perspective. For our purposes, often we can think of societal value as everything that is not already considered within the perspectives described previously. For example, the effective use of telehealth has value for payers because it may reduce per-encounter costs and give increased access to certain at-risk populations. It also provides value for providers by expanding their patient population they can serve, for patients who receive care they may not otherwise have received, and for the TPHO that provided the technology. Separate from all of those sources of value, potential additional value is realized when the patient becomes more productive at work. This type of value does not fit nicely into any of the other perspectives, but we can think of increased economic output as societal value.

We should also explore how individuals and organizations with these different perspectives view health, health care, the delivery of care services, and the goals they are intrinsically and financially incentivized to pursue or promote. This can

Table 1.1 Incentives of the different perspectives from which we can assess value

Perspective	Incentives
Payers	Payers are primarily incentivized to promote population health since the better the overall health as a community, the less need there is for utilization of care which reflects costs to payers
Providers	This group is primarily incentivized to improve the quality and efficiency of care delivery, but it also operates under constraints related to budget (i.e., they need to stay in business) as well as regulatory policy and oversight
Clinicians	Often clinicians' incentives will be aligned with those of providers described above and therefore they will be considered to share the same perspective. However, in some situations, incentives may be slightly different than that of, say, administrators (i.e., perhaps when advocating for a patient treatment that may not be financially responsible for the facility). Even when clinician incentives are aligned with the more encompassing "provider" group, we may wish to consider the clinician perspective specifically, such as in the example of the value of reducing clinician burnout
Patients	Patients have a vested interest in their overall health (population health) and the care they receive (care delivery) but are incentivized by both monetary and nonmonetary components. That is, to a certain extent they are influenced by the cost of goods or services that either promote staying healthy (e.g., gym membership, vitamin supplements, etc.) or treat illness (e.g., a surgery, medications, etc.), but they also are subjected to components that are often referred to as their "quality of life," "care experience," or other similar concepts. Basically, there's inherent value in feeling good and being healthy, and there's also value tied up in the cost of treating illness
TPHOs	The primary incentive for this group is not as easily defined. Clearly, as for-profit companies they seek out specific gaps in care they believe can be improved through a specific type of innovation, and they receive financial compensation for providing this innovation. However, that innovation may ultimately increase or decrease value for providers, payers, patients, or all three. For example, a high-functioning software is likely intended to benefit providers through more efficient and accurate care delivery and facility operations, while a digital wearable medical device may be intended to benefit payers and patients through improved population health. A device that allows for more complete vessel decalcification clearly benefits patients and providers, but it also likely benefits payers because it reduces the risk and rate of subsequent complications that would require additional care utilization. A discussion of how these TPHOs can ultimately capture the most value follows later in the book, but at this point it is enough to recognize that value from the perspective of a TPHO may flow from improvements in either care delivery or population health
Society	In general, a societal perspective is incentivized to improve the welfare of the general population in the aggregate. This involves improving population health and care delivery, but also reducing costs, improving access, reducing disparities, and promoting overall well-being

help us conceptualize how these individuals and organizations work together or how they will react to different policies intended to promote value. Table 1.1 lists the perspectives and the incentives they have regarding the pursuit of value in health care.

As we dive more deeply into how each perspective thinks of value, we will see that while certain stakeholders are incentivized to improve either population health or care delivery, they do not always have all the tools needed to do so. For example, patients have intrinsic (nonmonetary) incentives to stay healthy longer and therefore improve population health, but they do not always have the full information necessary to make the best choices. Think about the conflicting information regarding diet and lifestyle choices, either in situations where the science and research continue to evolve and make new discoveries or where the information simply is not relayed (or misinformation is relayed instead, either intentionally or unintentionally). Additionally, patients bring to any situation inherent cognitive biases that influence how they process and use the information that is available to them. Similar examples exist for other stakeholders in the system, which we will explore in more detail.

1.2 Value Assessments

Because value is subjective and dependent on multiple factors, methods for assessing it vary considerably depending on the situation and the objective. While it may be impossible to establish one universally applicable methodology, a reasonable goal is to develop a framework to guide the selection (or development) and use of a method or methods that can be universally leveraged. That is, some common components of all value assessments and concepts should nearly always be considered and specified, regardless of the situation or the chosen application. To identify these, describe them, and place them together with some structure will hopefully bring some level of consistency and common vernacular across value assessments.

Most simply and generally, a reasonable definition of a "value assessment" might look something like this:

> A *value assessment* is the consideration or evaluation of benefits from one or more perspectives in light of or relative to the costs needed to achieve those benefits within a particular time period and for a specific group of individuals (i.e., patients).

This may be so general as to not provide much guidance for a specific application, but it includes some of the key components present in any type of methodology used. That is, value assessments are primarily comparisons of costs to benefits, however those specific costs and benefits are defined; additionally, as we will explore more fully, the assessment must acknowledge whose perspective—payers, providers, patients, THPOs, and/or society—we're measuring value from, as well as the scope of the assessment in terms of time and those involved.

Depending on the perspective and the type of analysis, costs may be monetary; but they may include other components, like time, effort, resources, attention, opportunity cost, and a host of other items. Similarly, in addition to the obvious benefits of increased revenues or reduced costs, benefits may include improved patient outcomes, reduced risk, life years added, productivity, efficiency, patient experience, market share, and so on. In each case, which costs and benefits are relevant and how they are measured and quantified must be a function, in part, of the

Table 1.2 Common types of costs and benefits used in value assessments

Costs	Benefits
Money/investment	Increased revenues
Time	Reduced costs
Effort	Improved patient outcomes
Resources	Reduced risk
Attention	Life years added
Opportunity cost	Increased productivity
	Increased efficiency
	Reduced waste
	Increased market share
	Increased quality of life
	Improved patient experience
	Improved brand or reputation
	Increased satisfaction

perspective from which they are viewed. And, how these costs and benefits are compared will depend on the particular methodology chosen. Table 1.2 does not contain an exhaustive list but serves to illustrate the variety in the type of cost and benefit that can be considered.

1.3   Illustrative Examples

1.3.1   Value-Based Reimbursement Structures

There are a variety of examples of organizations turning to value-based models to pay for care delivery as a way to align incentives and encourage "high-value" care.

1.3.1.1   The CMS Hospital Value-Based Purchasing Program

The Centers for Medicare and Medicaid Services (CMS) have a variety of value-based programs where part of reimbursement is tied to performance on a suite of quality metrics. In the CMS Hospital Value-Based Purchasing Program [2, 3], hospitals are evaluated on measures related to:

- Mortality
- Infections
- Patient safety
- Patient experience
- Efficiency

Different domains are weighted differently, and hospitals either receive a bonus or are levied a penalty depending on their performance.

Immediately, this type of program elicits a number of questions and requires several clarifications. If someone were to evaluate the value associated with this program, they should consider the relevant perspectives, including patients, hospitals, and the payer (CMS). If assessing the value for providers, we might decide that the relevant costs are those hospitals invest to try to improve the quality measures their performance is assessed on while benefits are the bonuses they would receive. But in reality, hospital administrators also probably assess the opportunity cost associated with not making other improvements to their processes or facilities, the added administrative burden, and the potential impact on clinician burnout and the subsequent turnover or productivity loss due to lower levels of well-being, and so on. Similarly, true costs and benefits to patients and the payer are likely just as complicated.

Knowing what should be included is not easy, and given that little to no guidelines exist for what's appropriate, the right answer probably depends on whether your interest is in extolling or disparaging the program. Numerous research studies examine how the program may unfairly penalize particular hospitals, unintentionally exacerbate disparities in care, or financially incentivize the wrong type of behavior. On some level, however, what is needed is a conversation about what type of value the program is attempting to promote, how that value is defined, and how its performance will be evaluated in relation to that definition. The lack of specificity poses tremendous problems for those charged with evaluating the program and designing future programs, because it results in time, energy, and resources being devoted to debates of the appropriate costs and benefits instead of focusing on improving care, increasing efficiency, and/or improving the patient experiences.

Additionally, an obvious benefit exists for CMS (and other payers championing similar programs) to be able to compare value across programs and over multiple years. The difficulties in doing this are related to the same complexities just described, and so no consistent comparisons are made. If standards existed for how to frame a value assessment, you could avoid comparing apples to oranges or at least limit comparisons to components that are shared across programs. Ironically, even if these types of programs produced immense value to most or all stakeholders, the lack of a unified method for evaluating and quantifying that value likely dooms the programs to excessive (though warranted) scrutiny for the foreseeable future.

1.3.1.2   Blue Cross Blue Shield of Minnesota

In May 2021, Blue Cross Blue Shield of Minnesota (BCBSMN) announced via press release that it had "funded investments in technology and practice support resources for four independent medical care organizations" [4] in the state. Specifically, BCBSMN partnered with a third party that had developed a web-based platform intended to improve care coordination while tracking specific area metrics.

According to BCBSMN, this platform "facilitat[es] real-time financial rewards for appropriate care coordination practices."

While details are scarce in the article, it sounds like monetary payouts are made for certain *processes* of care as opposed to for achieving specific patient outcomes. Obviously, BCBSMN and its partner have determined that certain practices are associated with benefits to patients that translate into cost savings for them as the payer and are willing to financially incentivize clinicians to perform them.

Here, as with the CMS example, you might be interested in using a number of perspectives to assess how much value this value-based program contains. Additionally, clarifying the costs and benefits you would choose to include in such an assessment could be a source of debate.

Of interest to many, perhaps, would be to compare the value of this type of model to others, including the many federal value-based programs. If we could perform such a comparison, we might learn which program components drive value for different stakeholders and use those learnings to develop future programs. While the premise for value-based reimbursement makes intuitive sense for many (pay for the quality and appropriateness of the care as measured by how patients do, not for the individual tasks and procedures that are done), evaluating their impact and underlying value remains a difficult task.

In these examples, we struggle with not whether value is contained in them, but how to best define and quantify that value so that we can evaluate the merits of the program to answer questions like, are they worth it? And, how should we leverage these types of programs in the future? If a standard framework for how to assess value existed, it would be possible to consistently compare the value provided by programs or (at least the components of programs) across initiatives, which may provide unique insight that could inform future activities and policy.

1.3.2   Funding and Acquisitions of Innovative Companies

When we speak of value in health care, we must also consider the value associated with innovation and progress and acknowledge an important perspective of value that lies outside of those typically considered—that of the investor or acquiring company. As with the for-profit payer, the prospective investor's motivation is obvious: to make a profit. As a result, while the value of medical devices and digital health solutions will always revolve around improving the quality and efficiency of care provided, we must weigh additional considerations regarding market share, competitors, and corporate earnings that are a reality for those looking to thrive as innovators in the device, med-tech, and digital health space.

New TPHOs are born every week, all competing for the attention of investors, acquiring organizations, payers, providers, and/or patients. The value of these new companies and their solutions depends on a number of factors; therefore, assessing that value requires considering multiple factors and multiple perspectives, but that assessment must be slightly different from how we would assess the value of a federal reimbursement program.

Specifically, in addition to the benefits a particular solution has for providers and patients, an investor or acquiring organization may also ask:

- Does this solution fill a gap in care that our solution currently misses?
- Would this solution give us a larger market share or increase market capture?
- Can this solution reduce patient attrition so that patients are more likely to progress (when appropriate) to our other solution(s)?

Investors and acquiring organizations may ask any number of questions directly related to the "business case" of the solution that may not be relevant for a value assessment performed for a different type of organization. As in the case of assessing the value of federal reimbursement programs, a standardized framework for assessing the value of health innovation would allow for more appropriate comparisons and signal to innovators the kinds of criteria that are important if they want to demonstrate value to investors and acquiring organizations.

1.3.2.1 Virtual Health Platforms

During the COVID-19 pandemic, virtual health platforms experienced an unprecedented increase in use and development. In addition to the value these solutions have for clinicians and patients, they offer potential value for TPHOs that have complementary or similar offerings and see an opportunity to harness that value. Some examples of acquisitions in this space include the following:

Doctor on Demand is a mobile app that provides on-demand visits with clinicians; in 2021, it was acquired by Grand Rounds Health, a digital health company that businesses use to benefit their employees. It can help individuals find the right care, including coaching and expertise for specific conditions and diagnoses. The acquisition of Doctors on Demand allowed Grand Rounds Health to supplement their offerings with the virtual health care sessions that had become ubiquitous and almost expected during 2020 and 2021; obviously, they felt that Doctor on Demand held significant value for them.

Zipnosis is another telehealth platform that provides access to clinicians to get a fast diagnosis for specific conditions. Bright Health, which offers insurance programs, acquired it. Bright Health can now venture into the telehealth space without investing the time or resources to develop their own platform. Additionally, with the technology they also acquire market share and brand recognition, which hold tremendous value.

In these examples, the value assessment the acquiring organizations made is likely very different from that employed by those who would evaluate the CMS Hospital Value-Based Purchasing Program, but they share certain characteristics. And as we will see, both could have been created using the same underlying framework that focuses on perspectives, defining value in a way that is meaningful and relevant, and establishing specific metrics.

Ideally, as an industry we will come to view value similarly with universal definitions and a shared understanding of the critical components. If we can begin to employ a similar framework, we may find that different assessments are more comparable and allow for greater insight that we can apply across a variety of topic areas and situations.

1.4   The Structure of This Book

This book is laid out in four sections. The first, **Understanding the Challenges of Assessing the Value of Health Care**, explores the characteristics of the healthcare system that overcomplicates attempts to assess value. These are presented under umbrellas of "complexity," "continuity," and "consistency" (or the lack thereof).

Chapter 2. Challenge 1: Complexity. Care delivery systems are complex adaptive networks. This chapter pulls from theories of complexity science, network science, and implementation science. The complexity inherent in everything we could seek to measure in health care means that sometimes higher levels of quality may not result in higher value for one or more stakeholders. Additionally, the rapid development of new treatments as well as technological advances (e.g., remote patient monitoring) makes it difficult to anticipate how care delivery will look even 5 years from now.

Chapter 3. Challenge 2: Continuity. The lines between care delivery and population health are blurring. As an industry, we are moving away from the notion of distinct and unrelated episodes of acute care to a more holistic view of managing health. We will discuss the "continuity of care" between different settings and touch on the topic of the home as the new site of care as amplified by the COVID-19 pandemic.

Chapter 4. Challenge 3: Inconsistency. As stated in this Introduction, no common definitions or frameworks for how to think about value exist. Different perspectives, situations, needs, and goals all influence what value may mean and to whom. This lack of consistency leaves healthcare professionals to use their best judgment for how to assess value or to apply rigid tools that may not be totally appropriate to their unique situation. Examining specific components of the structure and mechanisms at play within the US healthcare system will inform how best to create a framework that ensures we appropriately assess value for a given situation.

In the second section, **A Primer on Fundamental Concepts and Current Techniques Used to Measure Value in Health care**, we consider value as defined by economists by exploring basic theories and describing how they impact our ability to define and quantify the value of health and health care. This involves notions of economic efficiency, moral hazard, price sensitivity, and other key concepts. We further describe specific types of value assessments, how they are used, and their strengths and weaknesses.

Chapter 5. Key Economic Concepts and Their Implications. This chapter will explore economic theory at a basic level to provide a background for what "efficient" means to an economist, how the allocation of resources can become inefficient, and how this relates to the notion of value. This chapter will explore moral hazard, price sensitivity as influenced by insurance coverage, issues of fraud and waste, and the administrative burden associated with assessing quality and value.

Chapter 6. Current Methods of Value Assessments. This chapter will briefly describe cost-effectiveness analysis, cost–utility analysis, ROI, and other relevant tools, and explore strengths and weaknesses of each as well as situations where they are more/less useful. This chapter will explore current reimbursement policy and what economic theory says about how Medicare and private insurance are attempting to promote quality and value through the use of financial incentives.

The next section, **Practical and Human Considerations: A Discussion of the Real-World Motivations and Requirements That Should be Contemplated When Exploring Value**, briefly examines practical and human considerations relevant to our journey. Given that population health as well as care delivery are largely functions of human decisions and behaviors, we must understand not only what influences those decisions and behaviors, but also how humans' interactions with each other and the environment may impact change, improvement, and even value associated with health care.

Chapter 7. Practical and Human Considerations. This chapter explores the motivations behind performing value assessments from the different perspectives mentioned in this Introduction. It also explores notions of responsibility and assigned roles within the current system (e.g., how much responsibility should we assign patients to manage their own conditions and follow a doctor's instructions versus holding providers and hospitals accountable for patient outcomes?). An exploration of the role of behavioral economics (i.e., cognitive biases, choice architectures, etc.) is included to provide a broad understanding of how human behavior influences value and should be considered when we are developing and carrying out value assessments.

Finally, in a section entitled **How to Design and Perform a Value Assessment**, we will develop a framework for performing value assessments that can be adapted to almost any situation while still providing guidance for how to identify (or develop) an appropriate methodology for a specific situation. We will explore some real examples and demonstrate how specific tools may be used.

Chapter 8. The Value Assessment Framework. This chapter walks through the three components of a proposed framework: (1) define value; (2) determine costs, benefits, and metrics; and (3) interpret and communicate findings. This chapter poses specific questions like, "Value to whom?" and "Over what time period?" It takes a practical look at determining what is measurable, valid, reliable, and quantifiable. It discusses the role of data, expert opinion, and so on, and explores the implications of neglecting to quantify some of the value that occurs when health or healthcare delivery improves. Pulling from theories of behavioral economics, this chapter encourages the consideration of human factors to acknowledge limitations and potential biases introduced into value assessments. Finally, it describes how to think of the value assessment within the larger context of the desired outcome and encourages the reader to really consider what they want others to understand about the value they are trying to assess.

Chapter 9. Examples and Practical Suggestions. The final chapter explores real-world examples to illustrate how we could use the framework to assess and compare value across programs, patient populations, or initiatives. It also includes practical suggestions for how to approach different value assessments as well as offer ideas regarding standards that we could adopt that would allow for more comparisons of value across different areas of the healthcare system.

References

1. Seixas BV, Dionne F, Conte T, Mitton C (2019) Assessing value in health care: using an interpretive classification system to understand existing practices based on a systematic review. BMC Health Serv Res 19(1):560. https://doi.org/10.1186/s12913-019-4405-6
2. Centers for Medicare & Medicaid Services (CMS) (2021) Hospital value-based purchasing program. https://www.cms.gov/Medicare/Quality-Initiatives-Patient-Assessment-Instruments/HospitalQualityInits/Hospital-Value-Based-Purchasing. Accessed 31 Aug 2021
3. Centers for Medicare & Medicaid Services (CMS) (2021) The hospital value-based purchasing (VBP) program. https://www.cms.gov/Medicare/Quality-Initiatives-Patient-Assessment-Instruments/Value-Based-Programs/HVBP/Hospital-Value-Based-Purchasing. Accessed 31 Aug 2021
4. Hagland M (2021) BCBS Minnesota's collaboration leverages technology to support value-based care and payment. HealthcareInnovation.com. https://www.hcinnovationgroup.com/policy-value-based-care/value-based-care-quality-measurement/article/21225074/bcbs-minnesotas-collaboration-leverages-technology-to-support-valuebased-care-and-payment. Accessed 31 Aug 2021

Part I
Understanding the Challenges of Assessing the Value of Health Care

Chapter 2
Challenge 1: Complexity

2.1 Complexity

Many of the difficulties in assessing the value of care directly result from complexity in some form or another. First, the healthcare system itself is complex: Care delivery is a team-based endeavor that involves many types of individuals in multiple autonomous but interrelated roles. The decisions and behaviors that result when a patient presents at an emergency department (ED), visits a clinic, or is admitted to a hospital are functions of those individuals as well as the surrounding environment and even regulatory and administrative landscape. Subsequently, paying for health care (a notion of particular interest for anyone looking to assess value) is complicated in terms of who pays as well as how much is paid. All of this is laid on top of the complexity inherent in patient health and well-being, the interdependence of comorbid conditions and the connection between the body and mind, as well as practical considerations related to access to care, personal choices regarding healthy behaviors, and the role of family and informal caregivers. When considered together, we can clearly see how complexity represents a major hurdle for accurately and appropriately assessing the value of a particular intervention, product, decision, service, or other component.

2.2 The Healthcare System Is Complex

To say that the US healthcare system is complex would be a severe understatement. Regardless of the reasons for its current structure, the consequences of this configuration include unaligned incentives between stakeholders, asymmetric information between those providing and receiving care, and variability in care practice and management. In another time, we viewed healthcare delivery systems (like hospitals, clinics, emergency rooms, etc.) as if they were essentially assembly lines with inter-changeable parts and one-size-fits-all processes to care for patients. The episodic nature of care was exacerbated by increasing separation between specialties and insurance networks that directed members to specific providers and facilities.

Currently, we are learning new ways to think about care delivery systems and how care is provided. Viewing these systems as unique entities comprised of networks of interconnected but semiautonomous individuals allows for new insights into improving the quality and efficiency of care provided. Additionally, regarding our own health, we now better understand components such as the link between physical health and the mental and emotional aspects of individuals' lives, the role of sleep and recreation, and the impact of stress on long-term health outcomes. To understand value and appropriately measure and assess it, we must have a shared understanding of how patients, providers, and payers interact to treat illness and promote health. Within this understanding must be an acknowledgment of uncertainty that comes from the human factor present in all aspects of the care delivery process.

Examining the complexity inherent in the US healthcare system is aided by theories rooted in complexity and network science, as well as implementation science. We need to establish a conceptual model for what healthcare delivery systems (be it a hospital, clinic, ED, HMO, or some other type of delivery system) are and how they function if we want to be able to think about how they produce and experience value.

2.2.1   Settings Where Care Is Delivered Are Complex Adaptive Systems

The fields of network science and complexity science have wide-ranging applications in biology, physics, technology, and economics. They have been used to explain the interconnectedness of every form of life in a tropical rainforest, the social behavior and the organic nature of cities and corporations, and other real-life phenomena. These theories also provide valuable insight into the functioning of hospitals, health systems, emergency rooms, or really any facility or location that provides care.

At the most basic level, those who work within these care delivery systems will make decisions and perform actions in an attempt to carry out their duties. During this process, they will interact with each other, patients, and the facility (their "environment") while processing information they receive to decide what to do. Any system like this will typically have defined roles, hierarchy, and structure (different departments, administrative areas, etc.), as well as rules and norms that together may loosely define a working culture. If we were to imagine looking down upon this care delivery system during a typical day, we would witness quite a scene of activity. There would be countless interactions between these individuals and a continuous flow of actions all motivated by decisions that may be large (e.g., to recommend surgery or not) or small (e.g., what to have for lunch). If we were to then transport to a different facility or setting, we would see a similar flurry of activity, but the actors, the physical space, and likely the underlying structure, hierarchy, and culture would be different. That is, there might be patterns of decision-making and actions that we recognize, but there would also be unique aspects of the components of each individual system.

Care delivery systems can be thought of as "complex adaptive systems," or CASs.[1] A CAS is made up of many semiautonomous but interdependent individuals who are interconnected in a variety of ways. That means that the individuals within the hospital or ED have specific roles and responsibilities and make many decisions for themselves. But they also interact frequently with those around them, which can influence their decisions and actions. And, while a CAS describes how the individual members are connected and interact, the behavior of the system as a whole also depends on the surrounding physical environment, social and/or cultural dynamics, and internal and external forces.

Consider what happens when an ambulance pulls up to an ED with an unconscious patient. Once inside the doors, physicians and nurses perform specific tasks while simultaneously relaying information back and forth, giving and receiving directions, and determining what to do next. Perhaps a specialty consult is ordered or at some point the patient is sent to radiology or the catheterization lab or somewhere else, at which point more interactions occur and more decisions are made (Fig. 2.1). In this example, multiple components are at work that influence what happens, including the interactions between the individuals delivering care, the

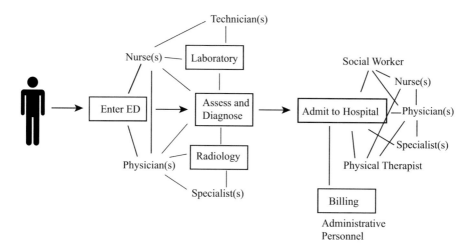

Fig. 2.1 The complex process of care

[1] Also referred to as a complex adaptive network, or CAN.

physical layout of the ED and supporting departments, how certain members may take more of a leadership role, or how others may defer to certain individuals based on previously established social or cultural norms, administrative pressures (budgets, regulations, etc.), as well as unique attributes of the people involved.

The complexity of this system is obvious since each of the network members must process information and make decisions while they also work with those around them to achieve their collective goal. The human element also adds to the complexity because individuals bring their own backgrounds, understanding, and cognitive biases to the decisions they need to make. We will cover this in more depth later, but for now it is enough to understand that these human elements influence the interactions with others as well as the information that each member encounters so that two individuals faced with the exact same situation and information may not make the same choices. Therefore, the system's function is dependent on the individual members as well as characteristics of the system itself.

The "adaptive" part of this system reflects the fact that the system as a whole can evolve and improve as the individual members continue to learn from their experiences. This is where innovation, research advancements, and quality improvement efforts often have a measurable impact on patient outcomes. However, not surprisingly these care delivery systems often struggle to implement and sustain real change within such a complex environment. In Part III of this book, we will look more closely at attributes of CASs and how the human element factors into the development and assessment of value.

The takeaway is that no two care delivery systems are the same. Even if similarities exist between them or they operate under universal regulations, they are unique in their member makeup, physical environment, social and cultural constructs, and so on. Therefore, when we consider value, we need to acknowledge that general learnings may not be applicable to specific situations and that measuring and effecting change (and therefore value) may involve different activities and strategies depending on the setting, situation, and individuals involved. When considered in this light, it is no wonder the underlying complexity of care delivery systems adds to the difficulty of accurately assessing and quantifying value.

2.2.2 Paying for Health Care Is Messy

We cannot talk about the complexity of the US healthcare system without mentioning the complexity of paying for it. Co-pays, deductibles, multiple insurances/gap insurance, coinsurance, public versus private insurance, health savings accounts, preferred networks, out-of-pocket maximums—the list of terms and concepts to describe the systems and processes of payments is extensive.

If we intend to examine value in health care, the financial support of care delivery is particularly relevant. Whatever course of action we pursue to improve care outcomes, efficiency, or experience, that action will often impact how much is paid by patients, providers, or payers. Therefore, we need to recognize that part of what makes it difficult to ascertain the appropriate value of changes or innovations is sorting what is paid, by whom, and for what. To further complicate things, charges and payments can change by type of insurance, the amount of previous payment (i.e., if a patient has already reached their yearly deductible), and who pays (insurance companies often have deals in place so that they pay less for the same thing than a private citizen would if they were paying out of pocket). So, whenever we attempt to include payer or patient payments in our value assessment, we need to acknowledge this variation and address the uncertainty it introduces.

Even if policy was enacted to greatly simplify how health care is paid for (e.g., a single-payer system or a fully public option), it may reduce the complexity of certain aspects of the healthcare system, but it would not necessarily simplify the process of assessing value. The simplicity or ease of measuring value would still depend on the chosen perspective and other components of whatever change, improvement, or solution were being considered.

As mentioned previously, healthcare policy has shifted over the past decade to include more "value-based" payments.[2] Unfortunately, these policies can sometimes misalign the incentives of different parties or may even undermine the success of well-intentioned quality improvement. An article published in *Health Affairs* in 2003 suggests that "misalignment of financial incentives creates a formidable obstacle to the adoption of quality interventions" and notes that initiatives can fail because of poor implementation, regardless of whether they would have been financially viable [1]. This suggests that even when attempts are made to financially incentivize certain behaviors, not all stakeholders may realize value and therefore this can inhibit advances in care quality. The implication is that many value-based payment mechanisms may hinder improvements in quality, not promote them.

The reasons may be in the underlying assumptions in place when developing and enacting this type of reimbursement structure. In a 2014 article entitled "Pay for Performance: Toxic to Quality? Insights from Behavioral Economics," the authors examine the underlying theories supporting pay for performance programs and lay out the assumptions these programs rely on [2]. The assumptions include:

1. That performance can be accurately ascertained; that is, measurements of clinicians' performance actually reflect their performance, not the nature of their patients, practice setting, or ability to game the system.
2. That the current payment system is too simple, suggesting that more detailed contracts rewarding specific, important aspects of performance will improve quality.
3. That variation in performance is caused by variation in motivation.
4. That financial incentives will add to total motivation, not undermine it.
5. That hospitals and physicians currently delivering poor-quality care should get fewer resources.

---

[2] Whether these payments are reimbursements for care provided and adjusted up or down depending on performance on quality metrics, or a capitated amount paid on a per-person basis depends on the context and situation.

The authors then claim, "under scrutiny, each of these assumptions appears flawed." The article goes on to examine each assumption in detail and describe when and where it breaks down. When viewed through the lens of CASs and what is true about such systems, we can immediately see that the assumptions the authors listed will rarely be valid within a CAS. Instead, the decisions and behavior of providers in a CAS will be influenced by a number of factors and cannot be explained or incentivized by a single factor such as payment.

Additionally, the complexity of payment mechanisms can complicate and even hinder our ability to attribute the increase or decrease in value to the appropriate stakeholder or initiative. While some of this is inevitable, we can take care to make certain decisions that will specify the key perspectives for a particular analysis, thereby clarifying how the financial payments reflect value for a specific initiative or innovation.

2.3   Patient Health Is Complex

In addition to the complexity of the care delivery system and reimbursement mechanisms, patient health itself is complex. We now understand that the episodic care model that is perpetuated under fee-for-service (FFS) payment schemes is often unable to provide the best care for patients or support their family and loved ones. This disjointed care that separated diagnoses and treatment by organ system or body part often resulted in waste, inefficiencies, duplicated efforts, poor outcomes, and poor patient experiences. For a long time now, many have recognized an opportunity to improve the value of care by reducing or eliminating disjointed and episodic care. Initiatives to promote "patient-centered care," chronic disease management, and care coordination activities are attempts to address these issues and encourage providers to consider more holistic care.

Payers recognize that mental and emotional health can impact physical health and that to the extent that poor physical health results in more costs for payers, supporting mental and emotional health holds significant value in the short and long term. Evidence also shows that involving patients in decisions regarding their care can lead to better experiences and outcomes. We understand that instead of thinking of care as simply something that is done "to" a patient, the promotion and maintenance of health and well-being is something that patients should actively participate in. Concepts like "shared decision-making" and "patient activation" have become popular outcomes to pursue and laud.

This holistic approach to care may ultimately produce better care and outcomes, but it also complicates our understanding of how impactful any one individual component is on health and well-being. Not only might it be difficult to isolate a particular component to study and assess its value, but it may also be that when combined, the multiple components of health and/or health care do not simply have an additive effect on patient experience and outcome. If the combination of multiple strategies to promote and maintain health produces a multiplicative effect (i.e., "the whole is bigger than the sum of its parts") then it may be impossible to truly assess the contribution of any one component. In just the last decade we have uncovered the importance of social determinants of health in determining what happens to patients when they face an illness or acute event. Many suggest that these factors have *more* of an influence on outcomes than direct medical care [3–5]. Correspondingly, while the best strategy to improve patient outcomes may be to address social determinants at the same time we attempt to improve the quality of care delivery, it will be difficult to ascertain the contribution of each activity toward the overall improvement in outcomes.

Technological advances in data collection, remote patient monitoring, self-management programs, virtual health platforms, and others will continue to improve patient care and health maintenance; but they will also further complicate attempts to assess value. We must understand and acknowledge this fact if we are to develop and employ specific strategies for assessing value that are robust to these complexities.

2.4   How Complexity-Related Challenges Often Manifest When Assessing Value

While it may be obvious why the complexity explored thus far can impede our ability to assess value, there are common ways that complexity-related challenges manifest in practice: obtaining accurate measurements, determining who or what to attribute a change in value to, the reality that improvements may not equate to value, and the ever-evolving landscape that signals an unknowable future (Fig. 2.2).

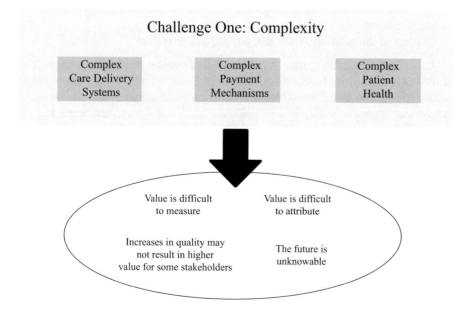

Fig. 2.2 How the challenge of complexity affects the ability to assess value

2.4.1 Complexity Makes It Harder to Obtain Accurate Measurements

Issues of measurement can be challenging in any setting, let alone a complex one. Value is subjective and often unmeasurable, requiring an adequate surrogate to bridge the gap between what we can measure and what we want to measure. For instance, asking a hospitalized patient the value of releasing them from the hospital a day early may elicit a variety of subjective responses rooted in an emotional, physical, or psychological basis. To measure that value in a meaningful way that can be aggregated and compared, we would likely need to have the patient fill out a validated questionnaire or provide a numerical rating of the importance of such an outcome. These types of measures may not exactly reflect the value the patient would offer without any parameters or restrictions, but they also allow us to assess value in a more systematic and quantifiable way. How well the surrogate measure(s) reflect the value we which to uncover may depend on the contents of the validated questionnaire or how easily a patient can theoretically translate their emotional reaction to a numerical scale.

Issues may also be related to how we measure information. Consider an example in diabetes care, where a process, device, or other solution is implemented to improve disease management. We know that measuring HbA1c values will provide insight into the clinical benefit produced by this solution and that specific targets for improvement—if achieved—can signify some level of success or significance. But what should we measure to assess the value? Some options may include:

- The number of adverse events related to poor disease management
- Patient satisfaction with the solution regarding its effectiveness and ease of use
- The amount of work the patient missed because of diabetes-related complications
- The cost of the solution to patients, payers, and providers

Any of those possible measures (and others, of course) can inform some aspect of the value of improved diabetes management: Fewer adverse events can improve patient lives and reduce the need for additional care utilization; higher patient satisfaction can improve quality of life and emotional well-being; less work missed means higher productivity and economic output; the cost of the solution may be relative to the potential savings it produces from the other metrics, and so on (Table 2.1).

Additionally, measurement itself is complex. Consider common examples encountered in research or quality monitoring programs:

Measuring 30-day readmission rates. At first, it might seem as though we can simply identify everyone who is discharged from a hospital and then count how many return to a hospital within 30 days. But some patients may have subsequent hospital stays that are completely unrelated to the index hospitalization, while others may have elective procedures that require a hospital stay. Even among unplanned

Table 2.1 Exploring possible measures of value for improving HbA1c in diabetics

Possible measures related to the value of improving HbA1c in diabetics	Relationship to value
The number of adverse events related to poor disease management	Reducing adverse events can: • Improve patients' lives • Reduce the need for care utilization
Patient satisfaction with the solution	The level of satisfaction can influence: • Patient quality of life and well-being • Sustainability/usability of the solution
The amount of work missed because of diabetes-related complications	Reducing missed work can: • Improve productivity • Reduce absenteeism • Increase economic output
The cost of the solution	The cost may influence: • Whether the solution is feasible • Whether patients would be willing to use it

hospitalizations, some are unavoidable and clearly not a result of care received during the index stay. Accurately measuring readmission requires that we thoughtfully determine who is eligible and what type of stay should constitute a readmission. We also need to consider how to account for differences in the severity of illness during the index hospitalization, comorbidity burden, social determinants, and countless other factors. Very quickly the seemingly straightforward metric of 30-day readmission becomes much more complicated, all because of the complex nature of health and health care.

Measuring patient adherence and persistence to a home-based therapy (like medication). One might try to measure adherence in multiple ways, including the frequency and consistency of prescription refills, self-reported adherence, use of electronic pill boxes that track when they are opened, even blood tests to assess the level of medication in a person's system. But none of these methods are perfect or always feasible.

Ironically, even though each patient will generate terabytes of data during their lifetime, we often struggle to find the right measurement for the right situation, with little recourse.

Knowing what to measure and how to measure it can be difficult because of the complexity inherent in the healthcare system and the multifaceted interactions between clinicians, patients, administrators, and payers as well as the underlying health of the individuals affected; the underlying health includes their comorbid conditions as well as their mental and emotional health. More than likely, there is no "right" answer regarding what should be measured to assess value because it will depend on the situation, the audience, and the goal of the assessment.

2.4.2 Complexity Makes It Harder to Determine Attribution

Ascertaining how much change or improvement can be attributed to a particular activity or process is always a challenge in health care. Randomized controlled trials (RCTs) are considered the gold standard for measuring the clinical efficacy of treatments precisely because they attempt to remove or control much of the inherent variability present in the practice of delivering care and health management. Yet, RCTs may fail to accurately demonstrate how the treatment performs in a "real-world" setting. Those in an RCT meet specific inclusion and exclusion criteria and are aware that they are part of a study where components of their health or lack thereof will be measured and compared to others. Often, RCTs exclude patients with heavier disease burdens or with limited cognitive or physical functioning so that the results obtained may not be relevant or generalizable to all patients.

Conversely, quality improvement activities are often conducted in real-world settings and therefore may provide a full picture of their effectiveness in everyday care delivery. But these activities often coincide with other improvement efforts, policy changes, audits, turnover, changes in leadership, existing trends, and other circumstances common to everyday care delivery activities. Attributing observed changes in staff performance or patient outcomes is frequently challenging, even when employing valid and reliable measurements.

At best, we may be able to estimate how much of a change or improvement can be attributed to a particular activity or process and/or for how long. But we may never be certain of the extent to which a cause-and-effect relationship exists. Further, because of the myriad of situational characteristics, we may struggle to know to what extent our results can truly be generalized, scaled, or transferred to another setting or patient population. This makes assigning value that much harder since attribution is key to determining the contribution to value.

2.4.3 Improvements in Quality May Not Result in Higher Value for One or More Stakeholders

I have written elsewhere that "quality and value are linked; quality and financial return may not." I expect that most, if not all, who read that would accept it as true. That is, most can quickly imagine a scenario in which that is true: Perhaps a hospital invests money and resources to improve the frequency with which clinicians remember to discuss smoking cessation counseling with current smokers or to improve materials intended to connect discharging patients to available community resources. In both cases, many would think those efforts reflect improvements in patient care but that neither likely would produce a monetary benefit for the specific hospital. And, because their costs were nonzero (whether you measure that in terms of money, time, or resources), the net financial return for the hospital is negative.

To extend the potential discordance between quality and return to that of value more generally (as opposed to strictly financial return) requires the qualifier of "for one or more stakeholders." That is, improvements in quality may not result in higher value for one or more stakeholders. In the previous examples of smoking cessation counseling and referral to community resources, higher levels of quality related to those services result in higher value for patients (as well as probably for payers because of the link to better future patient outcomes and for society in general). Whether it results in higher value for the provider may depend on how value is defined and measured, but it is possible that it will not. So, value increases when quality improves—but potentially not for all stakeholders.

This is one of the critiques of some federal quality monitoring programs. Some argue that imposing a set of quality metrics on clinicians or facilities may result in value for patients and/or payers but not necessarily for the clinicians or facilities. Even when reimbursement bonuses are offered for achieving certain performance levels, the financial payments may not reflect enough value to cover the investments of time, resources, and budget by that clinician or facility. Additionally, it may fail to recognize the opportunity cost of focusing on the prescribed list of quality measures in lieu of other investments the facility could make. Perhaps for some providers the investments put toward the prescribed quality measures would have produced more value (for any or all stakeholders) if used to achieve different ends, and perhaps the providers themselves are best positioned to determine how best to direct those investments.

Given the complex nature of care delivery, attempts to increase value in the aggregate or from a particular perspective may have negative consequences for individual stakeholders.

2.4.4 Complexity Contributes to an Unknowable Future

Uncertainty plays a key role when individuals face choices about health and health care. At the time of this writing, the world is embroiled in the COVID-19 pandemic, but with vaccines widely available for most ages including children as young as 5 years old. Personal opinions and politics aside, we can learn quite a bit about how uncertainty complicates health-related choices by exploring the thought process of a parent who might be debating whether to vaccinate their child. In addition to considering information that is known and has been proven clinically, the parent will also weigh components of uncertainty, such as "How severe would my child's case be if they contracted COVID?" "What's unknown about potential long-term or future effects of COVID for the unvaccinated?" and on the other side, "What potential side effects do I believe may be associated with the vaccine?" Clearly, if the parent had solid answers to those questions, they would have an easier choice to make. But it is not just about weighing one outcome versus an alternative; the uncertainty of those outcomes also plays a role.

In many cases, reduced uncertainty has value. In fact, to an economist, uncertainty and risk are essentially analogous. Reducing risk has value, as evidenced by people's willingness to buy insurance for their home, their car, and their lives. This willingness signals that most people value the reduction in the risk of financial or property loss more than the monetary value of the monthly premiums they pay. Investment portfolios that take on less risk also advertise lower returns, suggesting that those choosing them are willing to "pay" a premium (in the form of the lower return) to gain more certainty about at least a minimum return. In health care, patients and providers consider the risk of certain treatments as well as the risk associated with *not* treating certain conditions. Recommendations regarding regular screenings for certain types of cancers shift as new assessments emerge regarding the risks of the cancers as well as the risks (and costs) of the screenings themselves.

In today's healthcare landscape, rapid changes and development in treatments and technology make it hard to know what care delivery will look like even 5 years from now. The explosion of digital health, remote patient monitoring, wearable technology, and the interconnectedness of devices signals a shift in what will likely become the primary site of care (at home, virtually) and all that comes with it.

2.5   Summary

The healthcare system and components of patient health are complex and will only get more so as we continue to learn more about medicine and develop new innovations to treat disease and manage health. Therefore, the challenges this complexity poses, namely difficulties in measurement and attribution, will only get harder. This high level of complexity makes it impossible to have a single methodology for assessing value that is applicable to all situations and objectives. Instead, we need a framework that allows for flexibility and provides guidance for how to design a method that is relevant and applicable for each unique situation.

References

1. Leatherman S, Berwick D, Iles D, Lewin LS, Davidoff F, Nolan T, Bisognano M (2003) The business case for quality: case studies and an analysis. Health Aff 22(2):17–30. https://doi.org/10.1377/hlthaff.22.2.17
2. Himmelstein DU, Ariely D, Woolhandler S (2014) Pay-for-performance: toxic to quality? Insights from behavioral economics. Int J Health Serv 44(2):203–214. https://doi.org/10.2190/HS.44.2.a
3. Artiga S, Hinton E (2018) Beyond health care: the role of social determinants in promoting health and health equity. Kaiser Family Foundation, Oakland
4. Hood CM, Gennuso KP, Swain GR, Catlin BB (2016) County health rankings: relationships between determinant factors and health outcomes. Am J Prev Med 50(2):129–135. https://doi.org/10.1016/j.amepre.2015.08.024
5. Magnan S (2017) Social determinants of health 101 for health care: five plus five. National Academy of Medicine

Chapter 3
Challenge 2: Continuity

3.1 Continuity

The term "continuity" in health care typically has a specific connotation: the connecting of care delivered to patients across multiple settings and providers to achieve more continuous and complete care. While an appropriate goal that often has positive impacts on patient outcomes and satisfaction with care, this type of continuity can, in fact, contribute to the challenges of assessing value in health care. We observe this greater continuity play out in a number of ways: In addition to attempts to move away from disjointed, episodic care to this more continuous model, it also blurs the line between incentives to improve processes at the point of care ("care delivery") and a societal goal of greater population health. These reflect a move within the healthcare industry to a more continuous model of health management than we have pursued previously. At the same time, there is a corresponding evolution in our understanding of the concept of health as being more than just the absence of disease. That is, we can think of "health" itself as being on a continuum so that there are not distinct states (e.g., healthy vs. sick) and maintaining health involves more than just reacting when one falls ill. In each of these examples of continuity, what previously may have been separate, well-defined components of health and health care now often exist on more of a continuum.

The final relevant component of continuity for our discussion is the lack of continuity in health policy. The ever-evolving landscape of insurance structures, reimbursement mechanisms, and value-based incentive programs results in an inability to compare initiatives or innovations over time or even clinical topics.

C. A. Solid, *Practical Strategies to Assess Value in Health Care*,
https://doi.org/10.1007/978-3-030-95149-8_3

3.2   Episodic Care Versus a Care Continuum

As we move toward a more holistic view of health management and promoting good health, we also expand our understanding of how and where support for health can come from. While we previously may have sought out care only from "traditional" healthcare providers, we can now receive appropriate care from a variety of sources and methods. Additionally, providers themselves recognize the important roles played by other organizations. For example, peer mentor models have shown promise in better diabetes management and allowed for an easier transition back home after an inpatient psychiatric stay. Palliative care, addiction recovery support, and suicide prevention have all seen improvements through the efforts of organizations that are separate from the more traditional hospitals and clinics. These services and support offered by community-based organizations, nonprofits, and peer mentor services, coupled with advances in technology and the increased use of telehealth and digital devices, extend the continuum of care all the way from the hospital to the community to ultimately the home.

Those who wear digital devices to monitor heart rate and activity (e.g., Fitbit, Whoop, Apple Watch, etc.) continuously monitor their health and generate terabytes of health-related data about their lifestyles and behaviors; theoretically, that information could be used to make decisions about future care or health promotion. Advances in remote patient monitoring allow for more accurate and robust data in a variety of clinical areas, beamed immediately to providers for "real-time" data capture. While the availability of all this data should make evaluation of quality and value easier, it can complicate choices regarding what to measure—or perhaps more accurately—which measurements are appropriate for a given assessment. And the variety of technologies adds to the variability in the data that may be available for a particular individual or situation. Even if these are nice problems to have, they can pose challenges that didn't previously exist.

Despite additional sources of data, tracking patients and obtaining relevant data across all the potential sites of care (including the home) makes it more difficult to paint a picture of the full scope of care sought and/or provided. If data could be obtained from all the different sources, combining and reconciling them would require a mountain of time, effort, and resources, as each has their own system, process, data fields, and definitions that may or may not resemble those of other entities.

Paying for care across the continuum adds another layer of difficulty. Many value assessments rely on payer data to reflect costs. However, with multiple types of insurance, Medicare, Medicaid, health maintenance organizations (HMOs), accountable care organizations (ACOs), the Veterans Health Administration (VHA) system, and so on, the difficulty to obtain an aggregate of the care provided (and paid for) within a given population increases exponentially. As we encourage care continuity and collaborative health and disease management, we promote a reality where multiple data sources are required to paint the full picture of care delivery.

3.3 Care Continuity Blurs the Lines Between Population Health and Care Delivery

Striving to achieve high levels of population health while simultaneously establishing high-quality and efficient care delivery reflects a reasonable goal for any society. However, population health and care delivery are two separate components of that goal even though they are certainly linked. As the health of a population improves, its need for health services, treatments, and medications lessens. Conversely, the quality of care delivered to those who fall ill can impact population health (i.e., better treatment can result in more complete recovery, avoidance of reoccurrence or related events, etc.). But these two components differ in many ways and are influenced by different forces and from different perspectives, as we will see. Historically, much (if not all) of US health policy and structure focused on the component of care delivery, seeking to guide care practices at the site of care and reimbursing providers and facilities based solely on the activities that occurred at those sites.

The move toward value-based care is an attempt, in part, to fold accountability for population health into the pages of health policy that previously held providers accountable for care delivery. For example, hospitals are now accountable for how many of their discharged patients either die or are readmitted to a hospital within 30 days. These performance measures place the responsibility for these events squarely on the discharging hospital. This could be interpreted one of two ways. The first interpretation is that policy makers believe mortality and readmission within 30 days are directly and largely attributable to the care received by the individual during their index hospital stay and therefore these measures are adequate surrogates of hospital quality. The implication is that by improving the quality of care delivered at the site of care, these hospitals will impact patient outcomes in the weeks following their stay.

The second interpretation is that policy makers believe that hospitals *should* bear more responsibility for patients after discharge and therefore should implement steps to ensure patients follow discharge instructions, adhere to medication, and attend follow-up outpatient appointments beyond what hospitals currently have in place. Note that the first interpretation relates to care delivery while the second has a population health slant. My assumption is that policy makers believe that both are true and value for patients, providers, payers, and society will come from some combination of both interpretations, even if they may be uncertain of the relative magnitude of each effect (Fig. 3.1).

Casting aside for a moment that hospitals have rightly pointed out that numerous factors outside of their control can influence readmission and/or death within 30 days, let us consider population health and care delivery through the lens of value-based policies; this will allow us to see the challenges these policies impose. Specifically, we will examine how the financial incentives of different stakeholders can be misaligned—or even work at cross purposes—under a value-based payment structure.

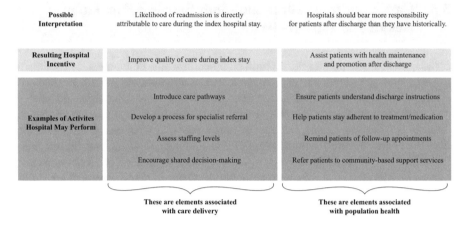

Fig. 3.1 Possible interpretations and implications of health policy that holds hospitals accountable for 30-day readmission

3.3.1 Incentives to Improve Population Health Versus Care Delivery

3.3.1.1 Payers' Incentives

Payers realize a financial return (i.e., value) from investments that improve population health because a healthier population will require less care that the payers fund. Therefore, they should favor payment structures that have at least some incentives intended to improve population health measures. This is likely why CMS quality monitoring programs include post-acute metrics of rehospitalization and mortality. What is not immediately clear is whether placing the accountability of these measures at the feet of providers is the most effective or efficient way to achieve higher population health. Private payers and employer group health plans have also increased investments (i.e., added benefits) into overall well-being, behavioral and emotional health, and lifestyle improvements. Presumably, this is an attempt to improve population health in order to reduce care utilization.

Typically, payers incentivize patients to seek care at centers of excellence and provider networks that offer high-quality care delivery; but in a fully bundled system, this motivation essentially relates to the impact high-quality care has on population health. The payer will (theoretically) reimburse the same amount to two payers of different efficiency because they are paying per episode of care or outcomes as opposed to reimbursing for the individual activities of care provision in a fee-for-service model.

3.3.1.2 Patients' Incentives

Patients are intrinsically motivated to have high population health (i.e., to stay healthy), but they face many challenges regarding the choices they make to maintain high levels of health. On a practical level, lifestyle choices and financial constraints may limit individuals' access to high-quality food or an appropriate diet, or individuals may simply lack adequate knowledge or information to fully understand what the right choices should be. Additionally, because of incomplete information (as described in Chap. 5), bounded rationality (Chap. 5), and cognitive biases (Chap. 7), patients struggle to make the best choice for themselves even under the best circumstances.

Also, patients are intrinsically motivated to seek out effective and efficient care; but they often lack sufficient information about either the clinical or financial components to be able to adequately compare options and select the most "valuable" one. The value for patients stems from the quality of the care experience (care delivery) and the impact it has on their health going forward (population health). Therefore, they need to weigh their care experience and the extent to which their health improves if they are to consider the overall value. However, the incomplete information they have to work with (maybe only a basic understanding of the underlying clinical condition, few metrics by which to compare providers, almost no knowledge of what any type of care will cost, etc.) and the fact that often they may not be able to accurately assess the impact care has on their overall health (a "credence good," as described in Chap. 5) makes it difficult for them to make value-driven decisions with any level of confidence (Table 3.1).

3.3.1.3 Providers' Incentives

Providers, under a bundled payment system, realize a financial return from improving care delivery processes while reaping no direct financial returns for improving population health. If providers can provide care more efficiently or cheaply, they "keep" more of the bundled payment they receive from the payer. It would be silly

Table 3.1 Financial incentives to promote care delivery and population health

	Financial incentive to promote better care delivery?	Financial incentive to promote population health?
Payers	Not directly, but indirectly to the extent that better care delivery translates to less care utilization	Yes, because a healthier population requires less care in general
Patients	Yes, but often lack sufficient information to assess quality or value of care delivery	Yes, but face challenges regarding the choices they make to maintain high levels of health
Providers	Yes, especially under bundled payment systems	Not directly, but some value-based payment mechanisms are tying some reimbursement to population health measures

to claim that providers do not want high population health, but from a strictly financial perspective and when taken to the extreme, a population that requires no health care would be financially ruinous to providers under the current system. Luckily, providers are intrinsically motivated to also promote population health through their sense of service and because of their interest in their patients' well-being (this is where the assumption that adding a financial incentive will make providers more interested in promoting health begins to break down).

Providers also care about their patients' care experiences but may lack input from patients regarding what they see as valuable (comfort, information, previous experience, shared decision-making, etc.). These days, some payers give providers a financial incentive to consider patient experience, as some reimbursement is linked to scores on patient-rated surveys like the Consumer Assessment of Healthcare Providers and Systems (CAHPS) survey.

3.3.2 The Expected Role of Patients in Population Health and Care Delivery

While improving the care and well-being of patients is often the clear goal of efforts to improve care quality and efficiency, the explicit role of patients in those efforts is rarely discussed or considered. Perhaps this is a result of our fixation on the definition of value as a function only of care quality and cost, which primarily involve providers and payers, not patients. Perhaps payers and policy makers feel that they have no direct influence over patient choices and instead believe that they know which provider behaviors to incentivize to improve patient health and well-being. Whatever the reason, reimbursement mechanisms and value-based quality programs typically ignore the role and responsibility of the patient in his or her own health and wellness. Yet, patients have perhaps the largest stake in ensuring they receive high-quality and high-value care.

So, what should a patient's role be? Where does the provider's responsibility end and the patient's responsibility begin? And what role should the payer play in improving value for patients? These complicated questions probably do not have right or wrong answers. But most would likely agree that the patient's role differs by clinical topic, type of therapy, and their own capabilities. The level of responsibility for improved health and positive outcomes is low for a patient receiving invasive surgery or who has limited cognitive or physical function; on the other hand, high-functioning patients instructed to follow a strict diet or adhere to a medication regime probably bear more responsibility for the effectiveness of the care delivered to them.

The point is that we should establish standards for patient roles and responsibilities and hold them accountable, but patients' involvement and influence on the quality of care they receive differs considerably in different circumstances. This lack of consistency (and the fact that it is unmeasured) complicates our ability to consistently assign value (and quality) to providers. Attempts to apply a universal method of measuring value would ignore this lack of consistency in the role of the patient and hinder the applicability and validity of those methods.

3.4 Individual Health Status as More Than Just Absence of Disease

As our understanding of medicine has evolved, we as a society have increasingly become aware of the difference between "not being ill" and "being healthy." That is, instead of simply seeking to treat and cure ills, we pursue health in the larger sense. Not only does the field of medicine continue to discover the complex interplay between different organ systems and body functioning (e.g., research connecting gut health to brain health), as a society we more frequently refer to a more "holistic" conception of the body and its well-being. Most people's understanding of conditions like addiction, mental health, and emotional well-being has evolved in recent decades, and as a society our expectation and appetite for these components of health have also increased.

This evolution coincides with the blurring of the line between care delivery and population health described previously. The two ideas have a natural symbiotic relationship: As we seek to promote health in all its forms and functions, we naturally think of the support of that health less in terms of episodic treatments and events and more in terms of health management. We want the different healthcare providers we encounter to communicate and share information with each other (usually); we understand the roles played by our lifestyles, behaviors, stress levels, choices, and surroundings on our health, and we want strategies for maintaining physical function while maximizing our emotional and mental well-being. Ultimately, this likely reflects a positive shift in how we manage and promote our own health, but it certainly muddies the waters for those seeking to understand and quantify the value of particular activities or interventions that are often aimed at addressing only one component of health (Fig. 3.2).

The shift toward a more holistic understanding of health may eventually lead to a more refined measurement of the components of health or health overall; but the understanding that better health care and better health maintenance both lead to better health adds complexity to the process of quantifying and attributing value. For example, instead of simply identifying the frequency of acute adverse outcomes that require a health encounter and the utilization of healthcare resources, a more fully integrated (and continuous) health assessment would identify changes in emotional or mental health, stress levels, sleeping patterns, medication adherence, and so on. Undoubtedly, this would provide a greater understanding of the underlying causes of health and illness and allow for a more accurate and complete understanding of the quality and value of care; but it would also require additional tools and resources to collect. Precision in measurement of any quantity, including value, invokes costs

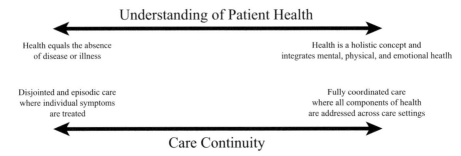

Fig. 3.2 The correspondence between more care continuity and a more holistic approach to promoting and maintaining patient health

related to collecting, managing, and analyzing the corresponding data. These days, one of the decisions now facing those who seek to perform assessments is whether each additional available measurement or datum adds value. When is it worth collecting information about mental and emotional health, and how should it be done? Yet, despite the increased costs, how valid are our assessments if we don't collect this additional information?

3.5 The Lack of Continuity in Health Policy and Payment

As with any large system, the rules governing the healthcare industry shift over time as priorities change, innovations are developed, and experience is gained. The current shift (a seismic one at that) in policies regarding payment mechanisms as an attempt to promote high-value care encourages certain types of value assessments and complicates others.

I often present the information shown in Figs. 3.3 and 3.4 to illustrate how the shift in health policy affects value assessments, and it is instructive to revisit it again here. Notably, the concepts these figures convey tie into the discussion of the relationship between care delivery and population health mentioned previously. As you can see in Fig. 3.3, historically, under an FFS model of reimbursement, a payer or government agency invests in some type of initiative or process intended to improve patient care. This may result in more accurate diagnoses, more effective treatments, more efficient processes, faster recoveries, fewer adverse events or readmissions, and so on. As a result, patients require less care and use fewer services, so that in addition to better patient outcomes, the payer sees a reduction in their costs because less care needs to be provided and paid for.

In a fully value-based or bundled model, the impact of the improvement in patient care will differ, as shown in Fig. 3.4. Specifically, any improvements in efficiency, accuracy, or treatment of patients at the point of care will produce value (i.e., cost savings) for providers since they receive the same payment for patients regardless of how they choose to treat them. This represents improvements in care

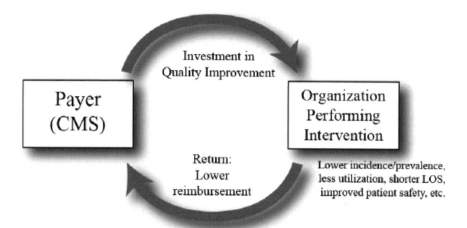

Fig. 3.3 Return on investment for quality improvement in a fee-for-service model (Reprinted by permission from Springer Nature: Return on Investment for Healthcare Quality Improvement by Craig A Solid ©2020) [1]

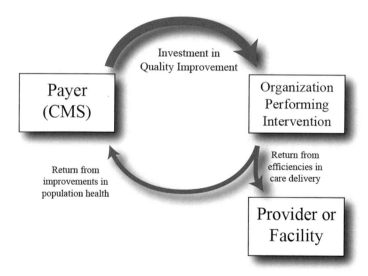

Fig. 3.4 Return on investment for quality improvement in a value-based model (Reprinted by permission from Springer Nature: Return on Investment for Healthcare Quality Improvement by Craig A Solid ©2020) [1]

delivery. What the payer realizes is now limited to the reduction in utilization that stems from improvements in population health.

The financial return realized by CMS is less in the value-based model than it was in an FFS model even if the quality improvement initiative generates the same amount of value. The financial value from the initiative is distributed differently under the different reimbursement models. Neither is necessarily better or worse from a value assessment standpoint, but we need to understand this difference when designing and performing assessments of financial value.

3.6   How Continuity-Related Challenges Often Manifest When Assessing Value

As with complexity, aspects of continuity (the presence or lack thereof, depending on the situation) impose specific challenges to assessing value in a number of ways, including, making it more difficult to isolate individual components of health or compare value across different settings, disease states, or payment mechanisms (Fig. 3.5).

3.6.1   Continuity Makes It Harder to Isolate Components of Health

As the lines blur between population health and care delivery, between the roles and expectations of patients versus providers, and between episodes of care and overall health management, we are less able to isolate and focus on any one component of

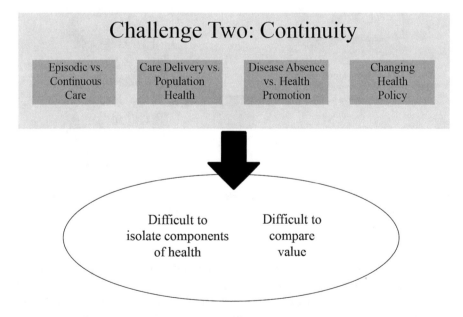

Fig. 3.5 How the challenge of continuity affects the ability to assess value

care. For example, we may want to examine a clinician's performance measure related to the care of diabetic patients to assess the value of specific activities in the care pathway the clinician provides, but the reality is that:

- Individual patients may play a significant role in their overall health and likelihood of diabetic outcomes, regardless of what their clinician does.
- Certain patients may be predisposed to poorer outcomes based on social determinants of health that influence access and timing of care.
- The general health of their neighbors and community can influence how patients view the healthcare system and its role in their lives.
- And so on.

It becomes increasingly difficult to ascertain the impact (and therefore the value) of any one particular activity or best practice without adding qualifiers regarding how all the other factors influence that endeavor. To assess the value of improving the hospital discharge instructions, for example, you would also have to consider whether there is a plan for a follow-up call by a nurse or case manager, the level of care coordination occurring across settings and with community-based resources, the social and economic factors that patient is being discharged back into, any community education or outreach being offered simultaneously that the patient may participate in, and so on.

In such a situation, it may be possible to assess the value associated with the entire suite of services and processes, but attributing value to specific components may prove too difficult outside of a highly controlled experiment. This is increasingly problematic when we want to determine the components with the biggest impact on value. We may understand the multiple factors at play, but we may want to know which factors are the most important to improve or invest in to achieve a certain level of value. If we struggle to isolate the roles different components play, it is not only difficult to determine how much of the overall value is due to each individual component, it may also be difficult to determine their relative impact; so, we may not know which component impacts value the most.

3.6.2   *A Lack of Continuity in Policy and Evaluations Makes It Harder to Compare Value*

Shifts in health policy and reimbursement, the implementation of dozens of quality monitoring and value-based reimbursement programs, internal and external financial pressures faced by hospitals and clinicians, and the varying incentives, financial and otherwise, all contribute to muddying the waters of comparison. We have no standard or established criteria for comparing value across clinical topics, payment schemes, or time periods.

Motivations for improved care delivery and population health that differ by perspective also evolve with changing policy. Providers have to adjust their priorities and refocus their efforts as quality monitoring programs and reimbursement programs shift how we evaluate and reward performance, and payers who seek to move to capitated plans implement different financial incentives to encourage certain care practices and promote population health.

Additionally, care that is offered and received differently by different individuals in different circumstances will inherently have indirect effects that cannot always be accounted for. For example, technology-enhanced care, which was receiving significant interest prior to COVID-19 but definitely received a boost from the pandemic, is increasingly touted as offering significant benefits to patients *and* providers. Various studies have shown that the improved communication allowed through smartphone apps and client portals improves patient satisfaction and increases "patient activation." This concept represents, in essence, the confidence and interest patients have in helping manage their own health and treatment because of increased information and empowerment. Studies show that patient activation is associated with better clinical outcomes and lower healthcare costs [2, 3]. Adjustments to health policy enacted to make it easier to reimburse providers for virtual care may unknowingly promote patient activation, which may in turn influence outcomes and costs. So, a comparison of an unrelated process or system before and after such a policy change may unwittingly compare different patient populations with the one post-policy change more actively involved in their own health and care.

Similarly, we may have previously established the monetary value of instituting a specific care pathway for patients receiving total hip replacement that reduces average length of stay and the use of services during the hospital stay. However, if that was established under an FFS model and we are now attempting to establish the monetary value under a capitated or bundled payment model, reimbursement is differently determined and therefore it will be difficult to compare any monetary savings to what we observed under the FFS model.

3.7 Summary

The shift from episodic, disjointed care to a more continuous model of health management means that the notion of value will be increasingly difficult to specify and therefore those who assess value will need to be ready to adjust definitions, methods, and perspectives to meet the needs of a particular situation or audience. Additionally, comparisons over time or to different interventions or disease categories become more difficult as reimbursement policy shifts. As the amount and criteria for reimbursement change, the financial incentives of various stakeholders also change. Understanding policy and its implications for various perspectives is key to ensuring that value assessments are performed adequately.

References

1. Solid CA (2020) Return on investment for healthcare quality improvement. Springer Nature, Cham
2. Hibbard JH, Greene J (2013) What the evidence shows about patient activation: better health outcomes and care experiences; fewer data on costs. Health Aff 32(2):207–214. https://doi.org/10.1377/hlthaff.2012.1061
3. Hibbard JH, Greene J, Shi Y, Mittler J, Scanlon D (2015) Taking the long view: how well do patient activation scores predict outcomes four years later? Med Care Res Rev 72(3):324–337. https://doi.org/10.1177/1077558715573871

Chapter 4
Challenge 3: Inconsistency

4.1 Inconsistency

The challenges in this domain stem from inconsistency in the language used to define and describe value and in the motivations of those seeking to assess it. These inconsistencies impede the development of a shared understanding of what we mean when we talk about value or make meaningful comparisons that could inform relevant decisions. In our exploration of value, we must understand how different perspectives view and measure value, as well as the different questions these perspectives seek to inform through informal and formal value assessments.

4.2 Inconsistencies in the Language of Value

Consider this major challenge facing health care professionals seeking to assess value: There is no consistent definition for "value." The inconsistency in the definition of value is not just a function of the multiple perspectives from which value can be considered (although perspective is important, as we will see shortly), because value is hard to define even among those looking from the same perspective. For example, if two clinicians are interested in the value of a novel treatment for their patients, one may look solely at cost savings or increased efficiency while the other may add in components of the patient experience or quality of life. This makes it difficult to settle on methods for assessing value and complicates attempts to compare value across settings or situations. The lack of consistency in the language of value also imposes an additional burden on those who seek to communicate value since even within a targeted audience several interpretations of what constitutes value may exist.

C. A. Solid, *Practical Strategies to Assess Value in Health Care*, https://doi.org/10.1007/978-3-030-95149-8_4

It is instructive to consider some of the different ways value is defined to illustrate the inconsistencies and set up a discussion of how we may begin to come together in a shared understanding of value.

4.2.1   Definitions of Value

Financial Value. One of the most common definitions of value involves some measure of monetary cost savings, increased profits, or return on investment. Cost savings and return on investment analyses are common measures of value used to establish the business case for decisions or activities. For payers and providers in particular, finance-based assessments of value are critical to determining whether activities are financially viable and/or sustainable. For third parties attempting to demonstrate value to payers and providers (or investors), the need to establish financial returns is paramount. However, even though financial value is often important, it almost never fully encompasses value from any perspective. Limitations of assessing value solely in terms of financial benefit include the fact that what is good from one perspective may be bad from another (e.g., a cost to payers might represent a benefit to providers) as well as the fact that many of the metrics we use to identify good care are nonmonetary, such as patient outcomes, quality of life, and overall well-being.

Patient-Focused Value. Given that health care delivery systems and devices or processes designed by third parties ultimately exist to improve how patients are cared for, a natural definition of value is one rooted in patients' experiences. These often include nonmonetary benefits like quality of life, well-being, satisfaction, and other "experiential" components of care. While these patient-focused outcomes may not result in financial value, they may provide patient-focused value through the experiential components. One of the most common measures of patient-focused values is the idea of a quality-adjusted life year (QALY). A life year is simply 1 year of life; if comparing the benefits of two different treatments for cancer, the one that is more effective at extending a patient's life will add more life years than the other treatment.

A QALY is a life year that has been adjusted for the quality of that additional year lived, reflecting the reality that not all life years are equal: Someone who lives a year with chronic pain, limited mobility, or cognitive dysfunction has a different experience than someone who lives a year in perfect health. In this way, analyses can consider not only the additional survival benefit of a treatment but also account for its impact on quality of life.[1] Some analyses, when comparing two treatments, will consider not only the difference in QALYs associated with each treatment but also the difference in costs of the two treatments. For example, if Treatment A

---

[1] The details of how to apply quality adjustments to life years are not important here, but we can employ various methods to attempt to establish the appropriate quality adjustment.

produced ten additional QALYs over Treatment B in a group of patients but cost $200,000 more to administer, then it cost $20,000 per QALY added.[2] A host of factors (that we will not go into here) influence whether it is worth paying the additional cost to get additional QALYs, but clearly, this process necessitates ethical considerations and exhibits a common conundrum encountered when considering value. The calculation of QALYs begins with nonmonetary aspects like extended life and quality of life but interprets the significance of the incremental improvement through a comparison of incremental costs. QALYs have also been shown to ignore the fact that patients do not always value things as we would expect (as we will explore in the chapter on behavioral economics) and sometimes engage in "hopeful gambles," as described by Lakdawalla and colleagues [1]:

> As a simple motivating example, consider one therapy—called a "sure bet"—that promises patients exactly eighteen months of additional survival. Now consider an alternative—called a "hopeful gamble"—that promises a 50% chance of thirty-six months of additional survival but also a 50% chance of no additional survival, or zero additional months. Both alternatives offer eighteen months of expected gain but may be viewed differently by patients.

In a study of hopeful gambles, these authors observed that 77% of those surveyed with cancer preferred the hopeful gamble scenario to a safe bet, suggesting that the hope of an extended survival may have value beyond simply its contribution to the average survival of a particular treatment. The authors conclude that "value should be defined from the viewpoint of the patient," and even claim that "economic theory implies that treatments should be allocated to patients who value the treatment more than it costs." This illustrates that understanding value from a patient perspective is anything but straightforward, and because value is subjective, any time we view it from a human perspective we must consider the human elements that influence that opinion of value.

Value from increased productivity or efficiency. For both payers and providers, measures of productivity or efficiency typically serve as surrogates of financial value. However, improvements in productivity and efficiency may also reflect improved patient experiences, reduced waste that may have led to adverse events, improved reputation or brands, or other kinds of value. They also carry inherent conundrums, like whether an identical intervention should be considered to produce more value among a working population (who will then presumably increase their contribution to GDP and reduce work absenteeism) than among retired adults (who will experience no such increase in output or work-based productivity). Even among a working population, income and wage disparities by gender and race complicate value assessments that consider certain productivity or efficiency metrics, like a reduction in lost wages or employment costs. And how should we consider the impact on volunteerism (which may be more common among retirees than a working population), informal caregiving, and the active promotion of social justice and

---

[2] I am describing the general methodology of cost–utility analysis, which we will cover in a later chapter; this calculation is called the incremental cost-effectiveness ratio (ICER).

equity? Certainly, there is value in volunteering, caregiving, and promotion of social justice and equity, but they may not be "productive" endeavors in the way that economists or actuaries typically consider.

In her book *The Real Wealth of Nations: Creating a Caring Economics*, Riane Eisler presents her perspective on how economics should be updated, noting that "we must give visibility and value to the socially and economically essential work of caring for people and nature" [2]. She goes on to offer multiple examples of how caring for people—whether it is a company caring for its employees or a government offering early child development—has produced tangible value by increasing productivity or individual capabilities. Her point is that caring for people and nature not only has inherent value but also often results in financial value. That is not to say that nonfinancial forms of value are only valuable when they lead to financial value. Instead, the point is that depending on the perspective and situation, a variety of ways to define and think about value may exist.

Sometimes, increased efficiency is related to a reduction in risk or uncertainty; having a more exact diagnostic test can reduce waste or duplication because of the level of certainty in the information it produces. Notably, one component of risk that can be included relates to population health: That is, there is not just value in getting better after an illness, there is also value in staying healthy. The most efficient promoter of health is one that maintains health and avoids illness before it starts. Smoking cessation is an obvious example; others include diet, exercise, stress reduction, and so on. Similarly, preventive methods that limit the severity of illness if it does occur (like how vaccines can reduce the severity of COVID) are also efficient: an inexpensive, low-burden activity (getting a vaccine) can greatly reduce the time, resources, and costs associated with treating someone who contracts COVID.

Emotional value. An increase in emotional value may result from patients' improved experiences or outcomes or from their opinions of providers or payers, aspects which are often referred to as improvements in "brand" or "reputation." As described previously, there may be value in providing hope to patients, all else being equal. There is emotional value in easing the burden of family members who care for loved ones in their home and help them navigate the health care system (both for the caregiver and the one being cared for). Proponents of advance care planning (ACP), including planning for end-of-life care, tout the emotional value of completing advance care directives and developing specific plans for care. Organizations that provide education and facilitate ACP, such as Honoring Choices, have observed the emotional transformation of individuals who go through the process and begin to get comfortable with tough conversations surrounding death and dying.

Social and equitable value. Social determinants of health play a crucial role in the level of health and access to health that people experience. Improving access to care and reducing or eliminating discriminatory or unequal care delivery has inherent value but also has been shown to produce financial returns for payers and society. Eisler, in her book mentioned previously, explores the "value of caring," where caring involves "empathy, responsibility, and concern for human welfare and optimal human development." These social benefits have undeniable value, and for an industry like health care, which exists to ease suffering and improve the quality of life lived, they seem like a natural fit alongside the other types of value already mentioned.

This list is not exhaustive, and others would likely name additional kinds of value or use different language to describe the kinds of value I have mentioned here. Leatherman and colleagues claim that a need exists to distinguish between the "business case, the economic case, and the social case" for improving quality. In essence, they see the business case as a positive ROI for a given entity, while the economic case may consider costs and benefits more generally and the social case may include benefits to patients and society in general. The differences between this description and what I have presented are mostly semantic, and the motivation is the same. The authors also note that the business case typically would not include important components like "philanthropic motives, regulations, or professional ethics." [3].

Another exploration of the various kinds of value is available from Lakdawalla et al., who are motivated to "broaden the view of what constitutes value in health care and spur new research on incorporating additional elements of value" into specific types of analyses within health technology assessments [4]. Their proposed list includes costs and QALYs, but it also includes other components like positive influences on patient behaviors, reductions in uncertainty and risk, and increases in hope and equity. The authors dive into some of the details regarding things like labor productivity, noting, "there is a growing body of work that has shown that elderly individuals, who do not usually directly participate in formal labor markets, contribute in informal labor markets by volunteering time for various activities (e.g., babysitting, counseling, and mentoring young people)." What an interesting concept: Better care of older adults creates value by allowing them more opportunities to help others through activities such as babysitting and mentoring. Putting the feasibility of measuring some of these components aside, it is a nice example of how differently we may define or construct value depending on our perspective and goals.

Still another perspective is offered by Anu Partanen, a Finnish-born journalist who immigrated to the United States and wrote a book on her observations of the United States as it compares to her homeland. When it comes to universal health care in the States, the focus is mostly on the direct costs and the implications for care delivery and quality, but Partanen's narrative invites a different take.

When commenting on the benefits of universal health care (as well as free childcare and free high-quality schools for all, among other things) she claims that providing these foundational services for all citizens is not socialistic but instead *promotes* independence and freedom. She says that's because it allows citizens to make choices about employment and lifestyle without worrying about the impact those choices would have on health insurance and high-quality care—something that is often impossible to do in the United States. As she describes the motivation behind these services,

All the advantages I gave up when I left Finland and moved to America—universal public health care, universal affordable day care, real maternity benefits, high-quality free education, taxpayer-funded residences for the elderly, even the separate taxation of spouses— were not gifts from the government to make me a servile dependent on the state's largesse.

Rather the Nordic system is intentionally designed to take into account the specific challenges of modern life and give citizens as much logistical and financial independence as possible [5].

It serves as another example of how value can be defined differently depending on perspective and frame of reference.

Regardless of the definitions of value you prefer, no clear link exists between all the definitions that would allow for a singular value definition. As alluded to previously, this emphasizes the need for better understanding of how to think about and define value for a given situation since the perspectives and situations to which an assessment of value may be applicable are so vast and heterogeneous.

4.3   Inconsistencies in the Motivations to Assess Value

4.3.1   Value-Based Payments

A variety of motivations to assess value exists. Policy makers' and payers' attempts to link reimbursement to quality and value comprise one motivation, but unfortunately even among policy makers there is not much consistency in how quality and reimbursement are linked. These days, a variety of federal programs, including the Value-Based Purchasing Quality Reporting Program, the Merit and Incentive-based Payment System, Physician Compare, Hospital Compare, and others exist. The details of these programs are not important here; you need to note only that they are numerous and that some aspects of how quality is defined and linked to reimbursement are inconsistent across the different programs. Most use validated quality measures to rate and rank hospitals and clinicians that will result in high performers receiving more payment at the expense of low performers receiving less. Which measures are used and how they are combined and compared differs by program, which poses another problem: A clinician may be evaluated on the same measure from two different programs. This can be confusing because the programs may make comparisons differently so that the clinician's relative performance can be inconsistent across programs, and it can also doubly penalize those who perform poorly because they may lose some reimbursement twice for the same measure.

To assess whether these programs increase the value of care, we must not only consider how they function and their relative payment structures but also the impact of the additional administrative burden as well as the cost related to the time and resources spent to develop, test, implement, and monitor all of the hundreds of quality measures involved. It can be difficult to know where to even begin to assess how these programs have impacted (if at all) the value of the care that has been delivered since their inception.

4.3.2   Investments and Acquisitions

In private health care organizations and among TPHOs, the motivations to assess value revolve around the need to fund operations or the desire to acquire (or be acquired by) other organizations. Digital health or device companies recognize a gap in care that represents an opportunity to generate revenues and make profits, usually by providing better care and saving payers money while producing better patient outcomes. When pitching to payers or health plans, these TPHOs likely highlight the potential for cost savings associated with their solution and may even present an ROI analysis, complete with estimates for the time until the initial investment by the payer is recouped. In these situations, the value for the health plan is not simply through cost avoidance but also through higher member retention due to better patient experiences or access to high-quality care. Additionally, it is typically not just a function of how much money the payer may save; the timing of that savings also matters. Savings that do not accrue for a year or two are not as valuable to the payer as immediate savings or those realized in the current fiscal year.

These same TPHOs may also want to be acquired by larger companies that may have complementary solutions or that just recognize a good deal when they see one. In that case, the company looking to get acquired may also explore the value to the (potentially) acquiring company in the form of larger market capture. For example, if patients with a particular condition are commonly lost to follow-up or only a fraction of them progress to second- or third-line therapy, it is possible that an innovative solution may help keep them on the clinical pathway and make them more likely to seek complete care and/or additional lines of therapy. An example may be in the urology space, where patients can sometimes feel embarrassed by certain conditions and be more likely to simply accept a therapy that makes their condition tolerable or a little bit better. If instead these patients were willing to seek out the best treatment possible, it could mean additional revenue for an acquiring company with a complementary solution and for providers who treat these patients. These types of value are in many ways very different from those considered when implementing value-based payment strategies.

4.4   How Inconsistency-Related Challenges Often Manifest When Assessing Value

Inconsistency, like complexity and continuity, imposes specific challenges for assessing value of health and health care. Specifically, inconsistency makes it difficult to define and compare value across initiatives, settings, or clinical areas (Fig. 4.1).

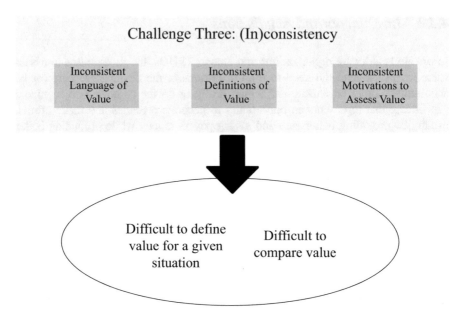

Fig. 4.1 How the challenge of inconsistency affects the ability to assess value

4.4.1 Inconsistent Motivations for Value Make It Difficult to Consistently Define Value

Quantifying value as a way to justify reimbursement is a very different motivation than quantifying value to inform decisions regarding facility investment or company acquisition. Those looking to incentivize providers to improve care quality in all its forms want to assign value to particular activities and outcomes and therefore need metrics that tell the story of what happens to patients and how they feel about it. Within reimbursement programs, there is inconsistency in how quality and value are defined, likely because of differing motivations between programs. For TPHOs looking to secure investment or be acquired, they need to measure key performance indicators related to volume, utilization, and efficiency. In essence, this distinction excludes the possibility of a single definition of value because it will ultimately depend on the combination of characteristics of the situation, perspective, and intention. This does not imply that we should give up on trying to standardize certain components of value; in fact, it could be viewed as the very reason why we should pursue some consistency. Maybe not all value can be compared, but if we are talking about the same motivating factors from the same perspective and for the same objective, shouldn't we at least be able to compare value in that specific situation?

Different motivations from different perspectives often impose inconsistent usage of scopes, including time frames and patient populations.

4.4.2 Inconsistent Definitions of Value Make It Difficult to Compare Value

As discussed, value means different things to different stakeholders and from different perspectives so that we cannot simply refer to "value" as having a universal meaning. Further, even when defined within the same perspective, functional definitions often differ significantly, which makes it impossible to directly compare results of value analyses.

No standards or guidelines regarding appropriate timelines or sources of costs and benefits exist; the true "cost" of care or a medication can vary wildly depending on who is paying and under what circumstances. Benefits from one perspective can be costs from another; patient well-being and quality of life are of interest to all parties but may not figure into payer or provider value calculations.

Perhaps the biggest surprise of all is that within large payer and funder organizations (like CMS), no consistent set of costs or benefits is universally applied across initiatives. Therefore, there is no reasonable way to compare value between initiatives even when they are funded by the same organization and cover activities occurring during the same time period.

4.5 Summary

While value is a core concept for much of progressive health care policy and reimbursement, we have no shared vernacular for how to talk about it. The lack of consistency in definitions of or motivations for value makes it difficult to be clear about what constitutes value. Further, we lack the ability to make meaningful comparisons of value across initiatives, disease states, settings, or time. If we ever hope to alleviate these difficulties, we must develop a consistent framework that still allows for flexibility and customization depending on the situation and objective(s).

References

1. Lakdawalla DN, Romley JA, Sanchez Y, Maclean JR, Penrod JR, Philipson T (2012) How cancer patients value hope and the implications for cost-effectiveness assessments of high-cost cancer therapies. Health Aff 31(4):676–682. https://doi.org/10.1377/hlthaff.2011.1300
2. Eisler R (2007) The real wealth of nations: creating a caring economy. Berrett-Koehler Publishers, Oakland
3. Leatherman S, Berwick D, Iles D, Lewin LS, Davidoff F, Nolan T, Bisognano M (2003) The business case for quality: case studies and an analysis. Health Aff 22(2):17–30. https://doi.org/10.1377/hlthaff.22.2.17
4. Lakdawalla DN, Doshi JA, Garrison LP Jr, Phelps CE, Basu A, Danzon PM (2018) Defining elements of value in health care-a health economics approach: an ISPOR special task force report [3]. Value Health 21(2):131–139. https://doi.org/10.1016/j.jval.2017.12.007
5. Partanen A (2016) The Nordic theory of everything. In: Search of a better life. Harper, New York

Part II
A Primer on Fundamental Concepts and Current Techniques Used to Measure Value in Health Care

Chapter 5
Key Economic Concepts and Their Implications

5.1 How an Economist Defines Value

Economics is a social science. At its core, it attempts to understand and describe behaviors and decisions of individuals as they seek to exchange goods and services either through bartering or the use of a store of value, like currency. Within the field of economics, the definitions of value typically reflect the price of a good, the amount of labor required to produce that good, or some intrinsic quantity that is subjective (i.e., individual "preferences" or "utility"). For the latter, methods attempt to measure intrinsic value, but the economics of efficiency, supply and demand, health insurance, public goods, price sensitivity, and moral hazard all inform an exploration of value more fully.

Within health care, we often think of economics as a means to assess the value of different health outcomes or the worth of specific policies or activities. This certainly has its place, but some of the most exciting applications of economics try to explain why people make certain decisions and how they view or react to specific situations. Obviously, this is relevant as we seek to assess the value of different healthcare-related choices, activities, interventions, or products. In this chapter, we will explore economic concepts that do just that as a way to better understand how to think about value in the healthcare setting. If we expect to perform an accurate and reasonable assessment of value, we must first understand the different components of the benefits, costs, and prices of care delivery and health promotion (Table 5.1).

A deep dive into economic theory unearths all sorts of complicated theories of value, many attributed to major economic personalities like Adam Smith and Peiro Sraffa. They incorporate concepts of marginal benefits, profits, rent, relative price, income distribution, and so on. If nothing else, they illustrate how numerous the definitions of value can be, even within a discipline focused on measuring and quantifying value.

© The Author(s), under exclusive license to Springer Nature Switzerland AG 2022
C. A. Solid, *Practical Strategies to Assess Value in Health Care*,
https://doi.org/10.1007/978-3-030-95149-8_5

Table 5.1 Some economic definitions of value

Type of value	Definition
Market value	The price or amount someone is willing to pay in the marketplace
Exchange value	The amount of money or of a good that is considered to be a "fair" or "equitable" equivalent of another good
Labor theory of value	The total amount of labor required to produce a good
Total cost value	The total costs of production (labor and capital) to produce a good

For our purposes, we will not be interested in one type of definition over another. As stated previously, we are not seeking a universal definition of value but instead how to think about value so that we can use the most appropriate definition for a specific situation. To do this, we need to explore some basic economic concepts.

5.2   Basic Ideas of Health Economics

5.2.1   Demand, Supply, and Prices

Anyone who has taken an introductory economics course has seen the classic figure of demand and supply, where demand slopes down from right to left and supply slopes up. In theory, where they meet is where demand equals supply, and this equilibrium determines the quantity sold and the price. The solid lines in Fig. 5.1 represent supply and demand, meaning the amount (or quantity) of good individuals would be willing to buy (demand) or sell (supply) for a given price. The demand curve is based on the idea that the lower the price, the more demand there will be for that good so that as price goes down, quantity goes up. That explains why the demand curve is drawn from the top left to the bottom right of the graph. The supply curve can be similarly motivated. The higher the price of a good, the more firms that find it worthwhile to produce the good; consequently, the overall quantity of the good available (the supply) increases. As the price people are willing to pay for a good goes up, the amount supplied by the market also goes up. Where the curves cross is where supply equals demand, and the "equilibrium" price and quantity are P and Q, respectively.

While that model is useful to describe the basic concepts of how changes in supply or demand can influence prices, reality is more complicated and those who are interested in the demand, supply, quantity, and price of health care tend to communicate using different concepts. As we know from our lived experience, most of us have no idea what the price of health care is—it is obscured by insurance plans and negotiated contracts between providers and payers. Often, more than one price exists for the same service; frequently, providers charge individuals a higher price than they do an insurance company that has negotiated a lower price as part of their

Fig. 5.1 Equilibrium price
and quantity as determined
by supply and demand

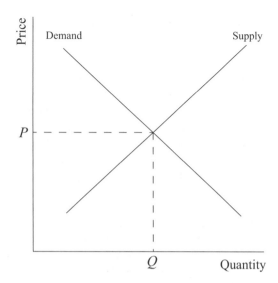

contract. Even within the world of payers, a private insurance company typically pays a higher price than does Medicare, for reasons that are beyond the scope of this book.

One of the key metrics payers look at is something called the "medical cost trend," which PricewaterhouseCooper's Health Research Institute defines as "the projected percentage increase in the cost to treat patients from one year to the next, assuming benefits remain the same" [1]. This quantity represents a measure that can be thought of as inflation as it relates to paying for health care. Each year's projection attempts to take into account current trends in care and utilization, disease burden of the population, supply chains, staffing, innovations, and other inputs. For example, the Institute projected a medical cost trend of 6.5% for 2022 (since 2014, it has hovered between 5.5 and 7.0% each year) citing impacts from COVID-19, investments in improvements and safety measures, and digital innovations in remote care as factors contributing to the cost trend. For payers in particular, the medical cost trend is one of the key economic indicators they use to plan for the upcoming year. An especially high-cost trend may signal a need to cut costs or increase premiums so that they can maintain profitability and pay for the care their members are likely to need.

Within specific examples, changes in the supply and demand of certain services will influence their price, which may or may not reflect changes in how individuals value them. Unfortunately, within a regulated system, real prices may not respond to changes in supply and demand as quickly as we would like. For example, as the demand for telehealth exploded during the COVID-19 pandemic, providers could not be reimbursed for offering it until governing bodies or payers implemented systems and codes for billing. Even then, the ramp-up of virtual health had its share of bumps and issues that were more complex than could be explained by supply and demand theory.

5.2.2   Utility, Risk, and Uncertainty

When economists attempt to model why an individual would choose one good or
service over another, they consider how much "utility" an individual experiences as
a result of a particular purchase or consumption of that good or service. Utility
could be thought of as value in a way because it is subjective, like value, and higher
utilities reflect individual preferences for things like pleasure, leisure, and time.
Some consider utility more akin to satisfaction, but in general it is a catchall for
what an individual "gets" when they decide to purchase (or not to purchase) a good
or service. For some analyses, utility is the measured benefit of interest as opposed
to a health-related event or patient outcome. For example, in a cost–utility analysis
(CUA), economists compare the cost of a particular treatment with a utility-adjusted
outcome like additional survival (i.e., QALYs). There are methods (discussed later)
to measure and quantify utility, but for now it is enough to understand that it is
intended to be a general metric of how "good" something is for a patient.

Utility is often used to compare the value of two different health outcomes. For
example, consider a patient with a chronic condition that affects aspects of their
daily life (i.e., maybe they have pain or physical limitations, etc.). An invasive treatment could improve their condition, but it may also impose negative side effects.
Which is a better or more valuable state? The one where the individual lives with the
limitations associated with the chronic condition? Or the one where that condition
is slightly improved but where the individual lives with side effects of the treatment? The answer depends on the severity of the chronic condition and the side
effects, but the answer will also be subjective. Assigning a utility to each state or to
individual disease burdens as well as side effects, we may begin to understand
which state an individual would value more. We can also compare differences in
that value to the cost for providing the treatment to identify a reasonable balance of
costs and benefits. This is essentially what policy makers and payers do when
reviewing a new treatment and determining under what circumstances and for
whom it should be covered.

There are also examples where a choice of risk is involved, as in a previous
example that discussed the "hopeful gamble" where individuals were asked to consider a treatment that would either produce additional survival or result in immediate death. Whenever these types of trade-offs are considered, the utility associated
with each option suggests something about the "risk profile" of the individual who
faces the decision. Someone who is "risk averse" prefers outcomes that are more
certain to those that are less certain, even if on average there is no difference in cost
or price. Let us consider a health insurance-related example to illustrate.

Assume, for simplicity, that there is only one illness in the world. Further, assume
that your chance of developing the illness in any given year is 10%, and if you do,
it will cost you $12,000 to treat. To an economist, your average or "expected"
healthcare-related costs without insurance in any given year are $1200 (calculated
as $12,000 × 10%). But, in reality, you would never experience a $1200 cost because
either you would pay $0 or $12,000, depending on whether you develop the illness

that year. Given this information, the amount of money you would be willing to pay for health insurance that would cover the treatment cost says something about your risk tolerance. The more you would be willing to pay, the more "risk averse" you are.

Think about how you would respond if an insurance company would be willing to sell you insurance for $1200 per year. Would you prefer paying that amount and having insurance? Or would you prefer forgoing insurance and taking your chances of having to pay out $12,000? Note that the "expected" cost of either option in a given year is the same: $1200. So, from a mathematical perspective, there is no difference between the two scenarios. But if you would prefer to have the insurance, you would be classified as risk averse because you prefer the certain outcome to the uncertain outcome, even though on average they cost the same. The more you would be willing to pay for insurance, the more risk averse you are (Table 5.2).

In Table 5.2, someone who prefers either of the insurance options would be considered risk averse. Someone willing to pay $150 per month for insurance is more risk averse than someone willing to pay only $100 per month.

Much of economic theory assumes that consumers are risk averse. Economists use this assumption to derive the equilibrium price of insurance and the expected utility individuals gain from having insurance. These derivations have influenced health policy regarding health insurance, as we will see.

5.2.3   Economic Evaluation of Health Outcomes

At the most theoretical level, health policy is an attempt to distribute healthcare resources (time, expertise, money, equipment) in the most effective and efficient way possible. Some would claim that the role of policy is to encourage the biggest benefit for the largest group of individuals. Inevitably then, we must place value on health states and outcomes to figure out which ones are "worth" the most to healthcare consumers. A variety of methods to do this exist, including:

- **Willingness to pay (WTP)**: To determine how much patients value an effective treatment to a specific illness or condition, researchers may ask individuals with

Table 5.2   Example of the calculated expected costs with and without health insurance

	No insurance	Insurance costing $100 per month	Insurance costing $150 per month
Probability of illness	0.10	0.10	0.10
Cost to treat illness	$12,000	$0	$0
Monthly cost of insurance	$0	$100	$150
Expected annual cost	$0.10 \times $12,000 = $1200	$100 \times 12 = $1200	$150 \times 12 = $1800

that illness or condition how much they would be willing to pay for such a treatment. For example, asking those with chronic pain, "How much would you be willing to pay per month to experience a 90% reduction in your pain, given that the treatment may cause you occasional nausea or fatigue?" This can inform what price might be reasonable for the treatment when it hits the market.

- **Ratings**: This involves asking individuals to rate where particular health states (various stages of an illness, etc.) are on a scale from (typically) 0 (dead) to 1 (perfect health). For example, asking those with kidney failure, "On a scale from 0 to 1, how would you rank living with regular kidney dialysis? How about living with a kidney transplant?" This may inform relative levels of utility for different health states, such as how much better patients might consider their quality of life with a kidney transplant versus having thrice-weekly dialysis.

- **Standard gambles (SG)**: This involves asking individuals with an illness (or asking individuals to consider an illness) whether they would prefer to live in poor health for 5 years or choose a gamble that would result in either an improvement in health or instant death. For example, asking those with limited mobility or physical functioning from illness, "Would you be willing to try a treatment that had a 90% chance of restoring your previous level of functioning if there was a 10% chance it would kill you instantly? What about if those percentages were 80% and 20%, respectively?" This can indirectly inform utility of the current disease state: The higher risk of instant death they are willing to endure, the worse their current situation must be for them.

- **Time trade-offs (TTOs)**: This involves asking individuals to indicate whether they would prefer a shorter life expectancy in good health versus a longer life expectancy in poor health. For example, asking someone with severe joint pain, "Which would you prefer: to live 20 years with full mobility or 25 years with moderate to severe joint pain?"

In addition to the obvious moral complexities of these exercises, are the considerable biases and inaccuracies they result in. A plethora of literature describes the cognitive difficulties of considering these scenarios and the potential implications on the accuracy and validity of their results.

There is also the issue of establishing a monetary value for patients' time, quality of life, and well-being. Classical economic theory usually considers patients' time in terms of opportunity cost; that is, the value of the time they spend out of work or unable to participate in everyday activities reflects the opportunity cost of either their wages (from a patient perspective) or productivity (from a societal perspective). Some studies attempt to use WTP methods to assign a value to leisure time and even unpaid work (e.g., volunteering).

The details of these techniques and the issues with them are less important for our purposes than the understanding that assigning value, monetary or otherwise, to health states, time/leisure, and outcomes is an inexact science. At times, we may want to forgo all attempts to monetize outcomes and express results in terms of the outcomes or states themselves.

5.2.3.1 The Value of Equity

Also relevant is a discussion about the impact of social determinants of health as they relate to health and health care. Most experts now agree that social determinants like housing, food security, employment, and education substantially impact the overall health of individuals. The World Health Organization states that social determinants "account for between 30 and 55% of health outcomes" [2]. Others, including the Robert Wood Johnson Foundation, claim that it may be as high as 80% [3]. Regardless of the exact percentage, most agree that social determinants of health may have *more* of an impact on outcomes than does direct care delivery. Therefore, from a value point of view they deserve considerable attention.

It should be no surprise then that employers, payers, and policy makers have recognized the value associated with health equity. The American Hospital Association released a brief in 2018 describing how disparities in access and care delivery result in poorer quality, more medical errors, and worse patient outcomes [4]. Addressing disparities to achieve more equity would have immediate returns in value. Some have suggested that more should be done to incentivize payers and providers to promote equity: A 2020 article in *Health Affairs* outlines three strategies for doing so, including developing equity-focused quality measures, adjusting payments and performance measures, and encouraging flexibility in how to address social determinants of health [5]. In the coming years, initiatives to capture value through improving health equity will likely continue to grow.

In addition to the value associated with improved patient outcomes and experience, there is significant value in equity from a moral and ethical standpoint. If we imagine a high level of population health, it is natural to assume that it would not include significant differences in health or access to care by age, gender, race, or socioeconomic status. In strictly economic terms, the value of equity is often established by determining how much inefficiency, waste, or productivity loss can be attributed to inequity. This should not detract from the notion that there is value inherent in equity but should help to accelerate efforts to improve health equity across the care spectrum.

5.2.4 Moral Hazard and Price Sensitivity

Of all the economic concepts covered in this chapter, likely none have influenced national health policy more than moral hazard.[1] The basic idea is that when an individual has health insurance, he or she behaves differently than if they did not have it. In previous writings, I have asked readers to imagine standing at the top of a ski hill with a difficulty rating that elicits some fear or trepidation and then to consider

---

[1] The term "moral hazard" is a bit of a misnomer because it has little to do with morality; in the broadest economic terms, it reflects a situation where one party is incentivized to behave riskily because it knows it is protected against the risk and the other party will incur the cost.

whether they would ski that hill differently if they had recently lost their health insurance. If the answer is yes (or if you can imagine why someone would say yes) then you just experienced moral hazard.

While this simple example helps illustrate the type of moral hazard that can increase the likelihood of future health care (ex ante moral hazard), what policy makers have historically been more interested in is the type of moral hazard that occurs once someone requires medical care (ex post). This type of moral hazard can be described through an equally simple example: Imagine that you are recovering from an appendectomy when your clinician walks into your hospital room to discuss your condition. She indicates that you can be discharged today and go home or stay one more night. She leaves the room, and you're left to decide. To check your options, you call your insurance company, and they relay to you that another night in the hospital is fully covered. If that information influences your decision about whether to stay another night, then you just experienced (ex post) moral hazard. Think about it like this: Imagine that a representative from the insurance company walked into your room right after your doctor left and handed you a personal check to fully cover another night in the hospital. They say, "This is yours. You can use it to pay for tonight's stay or you can go home today and just keep this for yourself." What you choose signals which you value you more: the money or the additional night in the hospital. If you would take the money, but in real life you decide to stay another night because it is covered, then that's moral hazard.

It can be hard to quantify what constitutes moral hazard in practice. Consider a situation where the insurance check only partially covers the extra night. You may value the extra night more than the money just handed to you but do not want to cover the difference, so you end up leaving the hospital and taking the cash. Or, what about a situation where you incorrectly assess the state of your own recovery and choose to go home when the clinically prudent choice is to stay the extra night? In that case, your perception of health and value results in the economically inefficient outcome. Strategies to combat moral hazard (discussed in the next section) are partially dependent on how sensitive consumers of health care are to changes in what they have to pay out of pocket for their care. But, their effectiveness is also dependent on how seriously care is needed: Increasing out-of-pocket costs may reduce low-acuity visits but may have little impact on hospitalizations or ED visits that reflect acute care needs.

5.2.5   Theories of the Demand for Health Insurance

Given the immense proportion of the US population covered by insurance (either private or public) and the influence these payers have on care delivery, prices, and utilization, it is necessary to explore the role of health insurance more deeply.

For years, economists have examined the reasons why individuals choose to pay for health insurance. For a long time, it was thought that this choice was largely driven by the concepts described previously regarding risk aversion and uncertainty.

Classical economic theory posited that individuals were risk averse and therefore preferred the certain expense of health insurance to an uncertain expense associated with paying for health care they may need. Economists' exploration of risk aversion and its implications have significantly influenced health policy during the last 100 years. Risk aversion as well as moral hazard have been driving forces in that policy.

There are others who are more adept at explaining these concepts than I am. In my opinion, one of the best summaries of the economic theories in this area is John Nyman's book, *The Theory of Demand for Health Insurance* [6]. Dr. Nyman provides an excellent summary of the history of different theories related to risk aversion and also points out where these traditional theories break down. The "new" theory he puts forth rebukes the notion that individuals buy insurance to avoid uncertainty. Instead, he claims that when individuals buy insurance they engage in a quid pro quo of paying premiums now in order to receive money later in the case that they are ill. He describes this as an "income transfer" at the time of illness from those who are healthy. The implications of this are wide ranging, but for our purposes, we are interested in what this tells us about individuals' behavior, including how and when they decide to seek care (i.e., "purchase" medical services) and how it may inform the value of these services from the patient's perspective.

For example, in the most basic model of health insurance, an individual would pay premiums and then when they sought out care they would face a price of $0, meaning that the services or procedures were "fully covered." Economists always get nervous when consumers face a price that is different from the true price or market price. That is, those services are not free, it is just that the individual does not pay for them, the insurance company does. This is the essence of moral hazard described previously: Since the individual who got the appendectomy would not have to pay out of pocket for tonight's hospital stay, he or she is more likely to stay, thereby increasing the healthcare expenditures by the insurance company. Insurance policies that include copays, deductibles, covered services, and preferred networks of providers do so in an attempt to influence the behavior and decisions of policy holders. The thought is that if those individuals have to pay out of pocket, even if it is only a portion of the expense, it may reduce the moral hazard. These policies work well in some circumstances but less well in others.

It is important to recognize here that real life is almost always more complicated than the simple example just described, however. In reality, private insurance options, plans, and programs vary widely; often, some services are fully covered while others are not, or certain types of services like annual physicals are covered but only once a year. Someone sitting in a hospital bed may not be sure what portion they will pay, especially if they have individual and/or family deductibles that they are unsure they have yet met, whether the hospital is in a prespecified approved network, and so on. The less certainty individuals have regarding what they may have to pay, the less influential these cost-sharing strategies will be on the individual's decisions and behaviors. Further, complicated insurance plans are not limited to privately provided health insurance. Often, public insurers like Medicare and Medicaid are supplemented by private add-ons (e.g., "gap insurance") and often collaborate or contract with private insurers through risk-based plans, like Medicare Advantage. In general, the landscape of health insurance has become so complex that it can be difficult to determine what portion of care is paid for by the different entities or what they represent.

5.2.6 Efficiency

For an economist, perhaps nothing is more sought after or satisfying than efficiency. Efficiency typically equates to things like minimum cost, maximum output, greatest welfare gain, or other "ideal" or equilibrium states. It is intended to reflect a state where all parties are as well off as possible, to the point where any additional improvement to one aspect would hurt another aspect, but, at the same time, nothing is superfluous or wasteful. Examples include: The lowest cost possible to produce a given number of goods; the fewest staff members needed to care for a patient without reducing quality; and the most productive allocation of resources to achieve the highest possible satisfaction. Efficiency is often thought of as the opposite of waste: Using more time, more money, or more resources than would or should be necessary.

However, the most efficient output is not necessarily the lowest output. For example, from a healthcare perspective, it would be inefficient to *not* spend money or resources on activities (e.g., treatment) that clearly benefit patients. In the hypothetical scenario where an insurance company delivers a personal check to cover another night in the hospital, whatever you would choose to do with that money would be the criterion for what an economist considered efficient in real life. That is, if in that scenario you would have chosen to keep the money, then in real life if you stayed the extra night in the hospital on the insurance company's dime, that is inefficient because you valued the money more than the extra night's stay. Conversely, if you would have chosen to use the money to pay for the stay, then in reality when you stayed, the insurance company's expenditure for that stay would be efficient. The former situation would be moral hazard, the latter would not (Fig. 5.2).

For our purposes in exploring value, efficiency refers to the "best" possible way to spend each healthcare dollar, where "best" is defined using specific criteria that reflect a desired outcome or goal. Often, it is more instructive to examine how circumstances or constraints can reduce or restrict efficiency to better understand what we should keep in mind when we are designing or carrying out value assessments.

5.2.7 Incomplete and Asymmetric Information

One of the first assumptions made in basic economic theories of price and the exchange of goods is that consumers are "rational" and have "complete information," meaning that they know of all the alternative goods and prices of those goods. The

What You Would Do If Given the Money Directly

	Stay the Extra Night	Go Home
Stay the Extra Night	Economically Efficient	Inefficient: You value the money more than the extra night's stay it pays for; the reason you are staying the extra night is because it is paid for (moral hazard)*
Go Home	Inefficient, but unlikely to happen, because if you value the extra night's stay more than the money you would likely stay regardless of who is paying	Economically Efficient

What You Actually Do

*The exception is if you incorrectly assess the value of that extra night; if, in fact, that extra night is the best medical option for you (whether you know it or not), then the moral hazard would actually be efficient.

Fig. 5.2 A graphic illustration of economic efficiency in the example where insurance will pay for an extra night in the hospital

assumptions of rationality and complete information extend into other theories and models of economic behavior, but unfortunately they may not often reflect reality.

Consumers do not, in fact, have all the necessary information to make the most "rational" choice. In health care, this manifests in multiple ways. The first is perhaps the most obvious: Often, patients do not know what is best for them. If a clinician suggests that they need a certain procedure or medication, the patient typically has very little clinical training or knowledge and therefore has no way to evaluate the recommendations on their own. (This is often referred to as asymmetric information: The clinician knows more than the patient about the services they are providing.) The clinician is thought to behave with the patient's best interests at heart, which can be a challenge unless the clinician fully understands patient preferences regarding treatment intensity, quality of life, longevity, religious or moral beliefs, and so on. If the patient is not forthcoming or is unconscious or unable to communicate his or her preferences because of some other reason, or if there is inadequate time, then the clinician may make decisions about patient care without full information about their preferences (Table 5.3).

Incomplete information also manifests through the reality that patients (and often clinicians) are unaware of the cost or price of much of what is involved in providing health care. Even with recent legislation designed to promote "price transparency" (the idea that providers of care list the prices of the services they provide), patients typically have no idea what a lab test or an X-ray will cost them or their insurance. Often, they do not even have a frame of reference—that is, whether the lab test or the X-ray will cost more, or how the cost at one facility compares to the cost at another facility. They also do not know how the costs of those lab tests or X-rays compare to the cost of a subsequent procedure if they decided to forgo the labs and X-ray now and risk the potential complication or illness later.

Table 5.3 Examples of incomplete or asymmetric information in the patient–clinician relationship

Examples of when patients have incomplete information	Examples of when clinicians have incomplete information
A lack of clinical knowledge about their condition	Do not know a patient's preferences for quality of life versus longevity
Do not believe the true likelihood of potential outcomes (e.g., assumes they will "get through it" despite medical facts to the contrary)	Do not know what a patient values
Cannot determine whether a treatment is helpful	Do not understand patient's social determinants of health, living status, access to care, etc.
Cannot determine which treatment will be or is more helpful	Patient is not truthful or forthcoming regarding symptoms, severity, healthy behaviors, etc.

Finally, even once care is provided, patients may not have full information regarding the benefit of those services. In economics, these services are referred to as "credence goods" and are described academically as "those whose qualities cannot be ascertained by consumers, even after purchase." We will discuss credence goods in more detail a little later.

The incomplete information regarding the cost or price coupled with the inability to accurately determine the utility associated with the care provided (the credence good) means that patients have almost no chance to accurately assess the value of health care from their perspective. Similarly, individuals may have difficulty assessing the value of healthy behaviors like diet and exercise or in taking preventive measures.

5.3 Potential Implications of Basic Economic Concepts for Assessing Value in Health Care

The economic concepts presented in this chapter should help you understand individuals' decisions and market behavior. For our exploration into value, all these concepts will inform how we will approach value assessments, and it is important to discuss some of the implications they have on how accurately and completely we can assess value in health care. While broken out in different sections as this chapter continues, there is quite a bit of overlap in the concepts.

5.3.1 Asymmetric Information Can Lead to Inefficiency

In the motivating example describing risk aversion, we assumed that the probability of developing an illness was known. In reality, such a probability is rarely known with any level of certainty. As a result, individuals may have difficulty discerning how much insurance they should buy or how to evaluate the value of that insurance. If, in fact, someone knew that their likelihood of needing *any* health care was extremely low, then health insurance of any kind would have little value for them, no matter how cheap. (This reality became visible in the earliest days of the Affordable Care Act, when very few young people bought health insurance, despite incurring financial penalties, because they perceived themselves to be at little risk for serious illness.) Further, when faced with an illness, patients have significantly less information than those caring for them and therefore typically cannot determine on their own the value of a particular course of action.

For example, say that you visit your doctor because you have some low back pain that has not gone away. Whether she suggests you have a scan, a test, some physical therapy, or prescribes you medication, you lack the ability to (1) compare the "price" of those different options or (2) understand the potential value each may have toward relieving your pain. Instead, you have to rely on your clinician's judgment and recommendations (presumably taking into account your general wishes, lifestyle, medical history, etc.). Even after you and your physician select a treatment option, your only criterion for its value is the extent to which your back pain subsided, and even then you may not know how much pain relief may have been due to the specific treatment as opposed to other factors or whether a different treatment would have been equally effective (say, physical therapy vs. invasive surgery). This illustrates why healthcare services are often referred to as credence goods. Credence goods are subject to inefficiencies because the "seller" (the provider) has an incentive to oversell (overtreat in health care) or raise prices because the buyer cannot tell the difference.

It should be noted here that some studies have shown evidence of this by conducting experiments where an otherwise healthy patient visits a number of physicians to see how often unnecessary treatment is prescribed. But, it is a leap to assume that when unnecessary treatment is prescribed it is done out of deceit as opposed to an error in medical judgment, an abundance of caution, or some other legitimate reason. In a real encounter between patient and clinician, a lot more is happening than simply the presentation of symptoms and a clinical diagnosis. Even so, it is easy to see how inefficiencies could emerge in the presence of a credence good.

Asymmetric information is also present when patients select where to receive care and by whom. First, patients struggle to accurately discriminate between different levels of quality, in part because of the same lack of clinical knowledge referenced earlier but also because available metrics may not fully capture true quality or at least that which may be of interest to a particular patient.[2] Second, patients typically have no idea what care costs (or should cost), so they are unable to make comparisons between facilities or health systems on that basis. Even with the recent implementation of a federal price transparency rule that requires hospitals to

---

[2] I recognize that CMS and other payers have instituted programs that attempt to provide consumers or patients with metrics they can use to compare provider quality; but even if those metrics were excellent surrogates for quality, the reality is that most patients do not bother to consider the metrics and therefore make decisions about which provider to see based on other criteria, like location, availability, and personal recommendations.

publish the price of different services, the information is typically difficult to find or understand [7].

Apart from the theoretical incentives credence goods impose on providers and the considerations that imply for policy attempting to encourage high-value care, most of the implications regarding asymmetric information relate to the patient's ability to determine quality, know price, and discern value. Therefore, when considering the value of care from the patient's point of view, asymmetric information implies that there may be difficulty in even defining the concept of value. Should we consider the value to a patient as that which he or she *perceives*? Or as the value that the patient *truly receives* even if he or she cannot accurately perceive it (assuming it is possible to determine it)?

For example, if assessing the value of a healthy diet and proper exercise regimen on acute cardiovascular events, you could clearly compare the monetary cost of that "treatment" to the cost avoidance stemming from the reduced incidence of acute cardiovascular events over the following year. More than likely, that type of analysis would demonstrate those behavioral changes as clearly having value for patients given the substantial detriments to health, quality of life, and perhaps even mental and emotional well-being associated with strokes and heart attacks. However, if patients were asked, they may only focus on the utility detriments of limiting their diet and having to endure strenuous activity, all to avoid an event they may not even experience. From that point of view, the assessment of value may look very different. This encompasses one of the main struggles of assessing value from the patient perspective: What is best for a patient is not always consistent with what they perceive to have the most value. Therefore, if claiming to employ "patient-centered" care, a provider needs to balance the well-being of the patient with that patient's preferences and perception of personal value associated with alternatives. It also assumes that a provider knows what is best for a patient including their appetite for invasive procedures versus palliative or end-of-life care. Unfortunately, these realities often make it difficult to assess value consistently across patients and situations.

5.3.2 Moral Hazard Can Lead to Either Less Efficient or More Efficient Use of Resources

Likely, you discerned at least some of the potential implications of moral hazard when reading the section that described it as a concept. Simply put, it suggests that having insurance could potentially increase the need or demand for healthcare services because individuals engage in more risky behavior. As nicely summarized by Nyman in his text, the traditional theory suggested:

> that because health insurance lowers the price of health care to consumers but leaves its costs unchanged, the additional care consumed by insured persons—that is, the moral hazard—is inefficient and represents a welfare loss by society [6].

The appropriate response to counter this welfare loss was to add copays and deductibles for consumers and impose oversight for providers to police the potential overuse of services.

Adding copays and deductibles makes sense in certain situations, like the example discussed previously about the extra night in the hospital. But, as Nyman points out, overwhelming evidence from research and real-world experiences shows that uninsured individuals are more likely to defer preventive health or even acute care than those with insurance, which suggests that adding insurance for these individuals would improve their health outcomes and therefore be a welfare gain to society (i.e., it would be efficient). So, based on Nyman's theory, the most effective policy would somehow reduce inefficiencies stemming from unnecessary consumption of healthcare resources but not reduce necessary consumption of healthcare resources that result from having insurance. He admits that this is difficult in practice but cites others who suggest a policy strategy where "severe, observable illnesses" have complete coverage, and when there are multiple viable treatment options patients would bear a larger portion of the cost if they chose one of the more expensive treatment options.

But even the argument for the efficient increase in preventive care is not cut-and-dried: Some suggest a danger of "excess prevention" in some cases, and it is not always clear what the appropriate cadence for, say, regular cancer screening should be. Note that regardless of whether policies and guidelines intended to limit screenings for low-risk individuals or those over a certain age are grounded in economic or clinical reasoning, in each case someone is making a determination of the *value* of the screening compared with its cost, either financially or clinically.

The other implication of patients experiencing a lower price of care is that they are inherently less sensitive to price increases. That is, if the price of a $1000 procedure is doubled, patients with a 20% copay, for example, would experience an increase of $200 (from $200 to $400) even though the true price jumped by $1000. This, in part, has contributed to the skyrocketing prices experienced in the US healthcare system over the last many decades.

5.3.3 Financially Incentivized Reimbursement Can Encourage Fraud and Inflates the Cost of Care Through Administrative Burden

It may be reasonable that a complex system like healthcare delivery has a complex mechanism to determine what hospitals and physicians are paid for treating patients. Diseases are complex and can often present with differing levels of severity; when determining the best treatment, clinicians must also consider comorbidities, risks of unintended consequences or side effects, patient wishes, and a host of other factors. But as the algorithms for determining payment or reimbursement get more complicated, it is more likely that opportunities for gaming the system or even fraud will exist.

These fraudulent activities may be as innocuous as adding additional notes to a medical record so that a different code can be included in a bill to the payer or they could be as severe as filing completely bogus claims. From a value standpoint, the possibility of fraud has obvious implications on the cost of care and the potential for overtreatment or mistreatment, resulting in poorer patient outcomes. But there is also a significant administrative burden to not only govern a complicated payment structure but to also police practices to identify and reduce fraud.

On a practical level, it may be rare that the administrative burden or the cost of fraud and abuse factor into the value assessment of a particular healthcare improvement or change; but it is necessary to consider for one hoping to fully understand how to think about value in the current healthcare environment.

5.4 Summary

Basic economic concepts provide a basis from which to understand how value has been defined and evaluated in the past. Understanding the motivations for health insurance and concerns about moral hazard shed light on health policy and the payment structures currently in place in the US healthcare system. However, we also see that many of the most basic economic assumptions, such as rationality and complete information, are clearly violated in real situations and therefore the theories built on them may fail to provide the best model for some situations.

An understanding of these basic economic concepts will allow us to more accurately develop a framework for assessing value and provide a foundation for healthcare professionals for how to think about value, economically and otherwise.

References

1. PwC (2021) Medical cost trend: behind the numbers 2022. https://www.pwc.com/us/en/indus-tries/health-industries/library/behind-the-numbers.html. Accessed 31 Aug 2021
2. World Health Organization (2021) Social determinants of health. WHO. https://www.who.int/health-topics/social-determinants-of-health#tab=tab_1. Accessed 31 Aug 2021
3. Manatt P, Philips LLP (2019) Medicaid's role in addressing social determinants of health. Robert Wood Johnson Foundation. https://www.rwjf.org/en/library/research/2019/02/medicaid-s-role-in-addressing-social-determinants-of-health.html. Accessed 31 Aug 2021
4. American Hospital Association (2018) Issue brief 3 connecting the dots: value and health equity. AHA.org. https://www.aha.org/system/files/2018-11/value-initiative-issue-brief-3-equity.pdf. Accessed 31 Aug 2021
5. Sandhu S, Saunders RS, McClellan MB, Wong CA (2020) Health equity should be a key value in value-based payment and delivery reform. Health Affairs Blog. https://www.healthaffairs.org/do/10.1377/hblog20201119.836369/full/. Accessed 31 Aug 2021
6. Nyman JA (2003) The theory of demand for health insurance. Standford University Press, Stanford
7. Appleby J (2021) Hospitals have started posting their prices online. Here's what they reveal. NPR News. https://www.npr.org/sections/health-shots/2021/07/02/1012317032/hospitals-have-started-posting-their-prices-online-heres-what-they-reveal. Accessed 31 Aug 2021

Chapter 6
Current Methods of Value Assessments

6.1 A Brief History of Value Assessments

The idea of value-based health and health care is not new. A quick PubMed search will identify peer-reviewed articles from the 1970s and early 1980s that explore the value of a human life [1, 2] in the context of determining an appropriate level of healthcare expenditure or for use in cost–utility analyses. Articles examining how best to control the volume of fee-for-service bills that begin to discuss value-based care appear as early as the 1990s [3, 4].

Further, the economic methods applied to healthcare situations have been around for much longer than that. Obviously, though, the shift toward value-based care began in the 2000s and was certainly spring boarded by the 2010 Affordable Care Act (ACA) and the 2015 Medicare Access and CHIP Reauthorization Act (MACRA), which established a mandate for an incentive program that tied reimbursement to quality measure performance. Much of the prevailing thought and opinion behind these legislative efforts are reflected in the commonly cited *New England Journal of Medicine* article "What Is Value in Health Care?" [5] which considered value solely as a function of outcomes per cost. Private payers have since expanded their value-based/risk-based models and programs, and the trend is likely to continue.

This push has coincided with (and is in part propelling) an explosion in quality monitoring and quality measure development. As programs linking payment to quality have expanded, so has the need to have valid and reliable measures of that quality. And, in a somewhat delayed response, program administrators and participants alike have realized that they must examine whether these payment mechanisms translate into higher value. Only in the last 5–10 years have value assessments gained mass appeal outside of the actuarial offices of large insurers. More and more healthcare professionals are finding it necessary (or at least helpful) to assess and demonstrate the value to help make decisions, secure funding, or justify activities.

C. A. Solid, *Practical Strategies to Assess Value in Health Care*,
https://doi.org/10.1007/978-3-030-95149-8_6

Therefore, the need to understand value assessments and the associated techniques has never been greater.

6.2   Types of Assessments

A number of tools are currently employed by those who assess the value of care delivery, processes, or investments in equipment or facilities. We will explore the most common tools and discuss their pros and cons and how they are typically used and for what purposes. As mentioned in a previous chapter, there is considerable variety regarding the methods used and even how those methods are applied. The summary by Seixas et al. [6] in their systematic review of value assessments provides an excellent synopsis of the heterogeneity of processes among assessors:

> All studies found in the literature review identify the depicted methodologies as strategies or frameworks for assessing value of health care technologies. However, only a few explicitly state their underlying concept of value. Some articles that report cost-utility analysis agree with Porter defining value broadly as "health outcomes obtained per dollar spent". Govaert et al. provide a similar but more specific definition of value in a paper on surgical auditing, understanding value as "the health outcomes achieved that matter to patients, relative to costs of achieving those outcomes". In the DCE experiment conducted by Green and Gerard, they sought to estimate the 'social value' of health care technologies, in which construct the notion of 'value for money expected from the treatment' is a component. It can be said that it represents an attempt to obtain a measure of allocative efficiency that rely on individuals' judgment on the evidence around technical efficiency. ASCO defines value "as a combination of clinical benefit, side effects, and improvement in patient symptoms or quality of life in the context of cost".

To summarize, the variety of value definitions in the studies reviewed included:

- Health outcomes per dollar spent
- Health outcomes that matter to patients, relative to costs of achieving those outcomes
- Social value, including the value for money expected from the treatment
- A combination of clinical benefit, side effects, and improvement in patient symptoms or quality of life in the context of cost

As mentioned previously, in addition to the number of different value definitions, the authors claim to have identified "22 distinct approaches" of value assessments in the literature reviewed. Obviously, a full grasp of all the methods used throughout the industry is elusive, but we should understand the basics of several formal methods, even if the details of how these are typically applied may vary by study and application.

6.2.1   CEA/CUA and QALYs

A cost-effectiveness analysis (CEA) compares changes or differences in costs to changes or differences in "effectiveness," however that may be defined. Effectiveness may reflect patient outcomes (extended life/prevented death, adverse event avoided, etc.), wait times, quality measures, or some other metric of interest to those performing the assessment. Most commonly, the ratio of differences in costs to the differences in effectiveness is calculated:

$$\left(\text{Cost}_1 - \text{Cost}_0\right)/\left(\text{Effectiveness}_1 - \text{Effectiveness}_0\right) \tag{6.1}$$

The subscripts are used to reflect the situations being compared, such as before and after an intervention, with and without the purchase of a new piece of equipment, or between two alternative treatment options. The calculated quantity reflects the incremental cost associated with gaining one unit of "improvement," such as how much a new treatment costs per death avoided. This is then used to determine if the change or intervention was "worth" it.

A common type of CEA is a cost–utility analysis (CUA), where effectiveness is measured by a specific outcome discussed previously: quality-adjusted life years (QALYs). As you will recall from Chaps. 4 and 5, QALYs are a measure of survival that are adjusted to account for differences in the quality of life. The more QALYs resulting from a treatment or intervention, the better it is, but not all survival time (i.e., life years) is considered equal. For example, if a group of ten people (say, a group receiving a specific treatment regimen) each live a year in perfect health, they produce a total of ten QALYs (Table 6.1). A different ten people who each live 2 years but do so with an illness or condition that reduces their quality of life to 75% of what would be considered perfect health, produce 15 QALYs (10 people × 2 years × 75%).

How quality of life is assigned to individual disease states and outcomes is complicated, but it is enough to understand that it is an attempt to quantify the reality that preferences for different outcomes are often a function of length and quality of life. An example is the comparison of different treatments for total renal failure: Either regular dialysis or a kidney transplant may extend a person's life, but one

Table 6.1 Examples of QALY calculations

	Group 1	Group 2
Number of individuals	10	10
Life years contributed by each individual	1	2
Quality of life of each individual[a]	1	0.75
Calculation of QALYs	10 × 1 × 1	10 × 2 × 0.75
Total QALYs	10	15

[a] Ranges from 0 to 1, where 0 = dead and 1 = perfect health

may provide significantly better quality of life and therefore should be considered "better" when incorporating it into the effectiveness of the treatment.

As before, the ratio of costs to QALYs is calculated (called the incremental cost-effectiveness ratio, or ICER), which represents the cost per quality-adjusted life year gained. Using this measure instead of a simple cost per life years added provides needed nuance to the value assessment and results in a more accurate, meaningful evaluation of the effectiveness of an initiative or treatment.

Extending our previous example, if the individuals in each group for whom QALYs were calculated were receiving different treatments, then we can calculate an ICER to evaluate the difference in QALYs relative to the difference in the costs of those treatments. Assume that the first group received the standard treatment, often referred to as "usual care," which costs $100,000 in the aggregate. The second group received a new treatment that claims to be more effective in extending life (which it seems to: Those in this group lived twice as long as those in the other group, but did so at a decreased quality of life); but the treatment that claims to be more effective in extending life is much more expensive: $475,000. Essentially, the ICER considers that it cost an additional $375,000 to gain five QALYs in the second group compared with the first, or $75,000 per QALY gained (Table 6.2). That allows policy makers or insurance companies to make decisions about whether the additional benefit justifies the additional cost.

Some analyses will refer to the method used as simply a "cost savings" or "cost avoidance" analysis. Often, these are simply informal or partial versions of CEAs. Perhaps a device company wants to understand the potential impact of reducing infections or improving access to care. They can perform an analysis to see what would happen to payer or provider costs if care were improved by a specified amount without specifying *how* that improvement would be made or how much it would cost. It can be a way to identify an opportunity for reducing costs or even provide guidance for what might be a reasonable price (cost) for their solution.

6.2.1.1   Usage, Advantages, and Disadvantages of CEA/CUA

Policy makers often use CEA and CUA to evaluate specific programs, initiatives, or treatments as they consider policy to incentivize different activities or decisions. One of the obvious challenges of the CUA in particular is the implication regarding

Table 6.2   Calculating an incremental cost-effectiveness ratio (ICER)

	Group 1: Usual care	Group 2: New treatment
Total QALYs	10	15
Total cost of treatment	$100,000	$475,000
Incremental QALYs[a]		5
Incremental costs[a]		$375,000
ICER		$75,000

[a] For Group 2 versus Group 1

the value of a human life. If one decides that a treatment that costs $75,000 per QALY gained is too expensive, then it suggests that an additional year of life is worth less than that. However, this also likely reflects the reality within which the healthcare system must operate. The article cited earlier and published in 1977 states it very bluntly when it says:

> "There is no way of avoiding the fact then, given scarce resources there is a finite limit to the value of life in health care." [1]

When making policy decisions, finite healthcare resources need to be spread across the entire population, and practical limitations mean that we cannot spend infinite amounts on any one individual. Therefore, it is perhaps better to think about CUA as attempting to consider the societal value of a particular treatment or policy, quantified and calculated on a per-unit basis.

In this way, often CEAs and CUAs can be directly compared across programs, initiatives, and even time periods. That is, the units are constant: Cost per unit of effectiveness, and as long as effectiveness is consistently measured and costs are adjusted for inflation (if necessary), one can make direct comparisons to arrive at decisions regarding which initiative or program was or will be more cost-effective. These types of analyses are some of the most common tools decision makers use.

6.2.2   ROI

Return on investment (ROI) analyses in health care is an area I have expanded on previously [7], and one that has gained significant favor across the healthcare spectrum over the last decade. If done intentionally and with sufficient forethought, ROI analyses can provide substantial insight for a variety of perspectives.

In general, ROI involves a comparison of the costs associated with a particular healthcare solution to the benefits realized. It calculates the return as the difference, relative to the magnitude of the costs, presented as a percentage:

$$\text{ROI} = \left(\text{Benefits} - \text{Costs}\right) / \text{Costs} \times 100\% \qquad (6.2)$$

The calculation and its interpretation are the same as you would make regarding any kind of financial investment. The primary challenge of ROI analyses lies in defining and quantifying the benefits and the costs, given that both are general terms and that they imply monetary quantities when much of what is important in improving health care is nonmonetary.

You must determine and define what costs and benefits you will include and how you will estimate or calculate them. This requires an assessor to clearly define specific parameters of the analysis, including the perspective (patients, clinicians, hospitals, payers, etc.) and scope (which patients, over which time period, including which activities, etc.). Because of the number and nature of the quantities involved, a complete ROI analysis always includes a sensitivity analysis where values are adjusted up and down to demonstrate the effect on the resulting return.

We must also acknowledge that much of the benefit of many care improvements involves concepts like quality of life, patient experience, satisfaction, and other subjective and elusive quantities. I recommend that when calculating the base case of an ROI analysis, include only those costs and benefits that are measurable, monetizable, and attributable (MMA) to the particular change, intervention, or solution. During subsequent sensitivity analyses, you may be able to extrapolate to include components that are not completely MMA; and within the larger context of the interpretation, you can (and should) expand on the non-MMA costs and benefits that the reader or audience should consider.

6.2.2.1 Usage, Advantages, and Disadvantages of ROI

ROI can be effectively utilized by providers, payers, policy makers, and even patients. They can use it prospectively to estimate future return to aid with decision-making and planning, or retrospectively to justify spending or identify key drivers of value that may inform how best to implement, translate, and scale activities for different populations and settings.

The variety regarding how to define and quantify the costs and benefits involved in ROI gives the method great strength and flexibility, but it also makes it difficult to compare results from different initiatives or care solutions, even if the definitions involved in each analysis differ only slightly. This is because of the compounding nature of many ROI analyses: You may have to assume several aspects, such as recruitment, effectiveness, cost, timeline, and so on, and the variability inherent in each of those assumptions will multiply when you consider them together. For example, if you slightly overestimate recruitment and effectiveness of an intervention, the results could be catastrophic because you have fewer people *and* a less effective intervention; together, the impact on the number of, say, adverse events avoided is larger than either incorrect assumption contributed to on its own.

A hypothetical example is shown in Fig. 6.1. In it, when estimating the monetary benefits of reducing falls, the assessor makes several assumptions regarding recruitment, the effectiveness of the intervention, and the underlying cost savings associated with avoiding a fall. When those estimates are varied slightly, they may end up producing very different estimates of the overall monetary value.

Additionally, it can be difficult to know what costs or benefits should be included, and there may be several of each that are difficult or impossible to monetize. This adds to the variability seen across methodologies claiming to estimate the return in some way or another.

Finally, there is variety in how ROI itself is defined. Some will define it as in Eq. (6.3), which is more accurately named the benefit-to-cost ratio (BCR) and represents the "benefit per dollar spent."

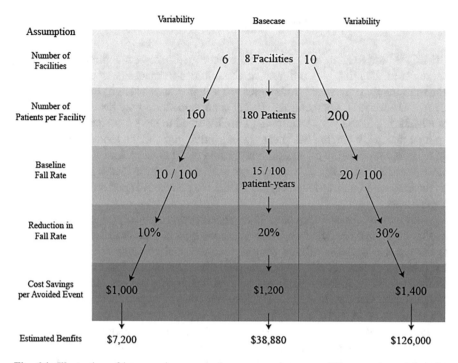

Fig. 6.1 Illustration of how varying assumptions can produce very different estimated benefits (Reprinted by permission by Springer Nature: Return on Investment for Healthcare Quality Improvement by Craig A. Solid ©2020) [7]

$$BCR = \text{Benefits} / \text{Costs} \qquad (6.3)$$

The main difference in interpretation of the ROI versus the BCR is the break-even point. The BCR equals 1.0 when benefits equal costs; situations that reflect a negative ROI (benefits are less than costs) produce a BCR less than one *but greater than zero* since it is a ratio. This can cause confusion for an uninformed reader: Referring to a positive value calculated as the ratio in Eq. (6.3) as being negative (as in "a negative ROI") requires either that you understand the difference between BCR and ROI or the error in the definition. Unfortunately, this type of mix-up is common in the existing literature on ROI.

Other metrics are often useful when conducting ROI analyses. The payback period calculates the amount of time until the accumulated benefits equal the total costs. Given that often changes or improvements in care have lasting effects, this allows you to explore scenarios without having to specify the time horizon needed to perform the ROI calculation.

6.2.3 Additional Methods

CEA/CUA and ROI are certainly not the only methods; as mentioned previously, Seixas et al. identified 22 different methodologies in their systematic review [6], although many of those methodologies are special cases or slight modifications of CEA, CUA, or ROI. For example, the net economic return may involve simulations of a Markov process where individuals are assumed to have a probability of developing a disease, incurring healthcare costs, and dying, and the model is run to estimate costs and benefits of a particular treatment. This has a lot of overlap with a more general ROI analysis, where inputs are assumed, estimates are created based on those assumptions, and some type of sensitivity analysis is performed to quantify uncertainty.

Additionally, frameworks have been developed specifically to evaluate cancer treatments and/or medications. These methods typically produce a "score" related to the types of benefits offered by the treatment and compare those to costs. As indicated by Bentley et al., "such frameworks conceptually define 'value' generally on the basis of treatment benefit and cost, although they use different components (e.g., efficacy, toxicity, and quality of life) and analytic approaches" [8]. Within the private industry of TPHOs like digital health and device companies, an important component of value from some perspectives is market capture and/or patient retention. Again, in almost any value analysis you will compare costs of some kind to benefits of some kind; the differences often lie in the details of what costs and/or benefits are considered, how they are measured and quantified, and how variability is addressed.

In general, there are as many different ways to assess value as there are to think about and define it. But, as stated earlier, a value assessment is typically the consideration or evaluation of benefits in light of or relative to the costs needed to achieve those benefits. As such, our goal is not to define a single methodology applicable to every situation but instead to develop a framework for how to approach situations where value assessment is needed to ensure that an appropriate methodology can be applied; this is regardless of whether that approach is well established or completely novel (Table 6.3).

Table 6.3 Pros and cons of common value assessment methods

	Pros	Cons
CEA/CUA	• Uses a standard metric (ICER) that can be compared across different initiatives or treatments	• May involve assigning QALYs which can be imprecise • Inherently assigns a monetary value to a human life
ROI	• Flexible in how it is designed and applied so that it is applicable in many situations	• Can be difficult to compare across analyses • Includes only financial return; excludes nonmonetary benefits like quality of life

6.2.4 Discounting and Risk Adjustment

Within many economic analyses, some topics merit a cursory examination because they historically have caused much confusion and consternation among those not well versed in their details. We will touch on them briefly here because they often appear in value assessments, but more complete examinations can be found from any number of other sources.

6.2.4.1 Discounting

The practice of discounting monetary values is well accepted and often expected if incorporating values from multiple calendar years. The general idea is straightforward: A benefit or cost of $100 realized today is worth more than $100 realized in a year or two. Therefore, to accurately represent the overall cost and benefit in today's dollars, amounts realized in future years are discounted to what they would be worth today.

This process is relatively straightforward, and, with minimal effort, you can find the details of how to appropriately discount financial results from any number of sources. However, many fail to realize that discounting can affect the calculated return rate or cost/benefit ratio if (as is often the case) costs and benefits do not accrue at an equal rate across time. That is, it is common for much of the cost of an intervention or change to occur up front (like an investment in equipment, training, or a new process), while benefits may accrue over time and at a changing rate (e.g., perhaps there is a learning curve so that benefit accrual starts out slowly and increases over time, or conversely perhaps the largest benefit from staff training occurs right away and wanes over time as the training is forgotten).

An example pulled from my most recent book is reprinted here, where benefits of $2500 per year for 3 years are compared to initial costs of $4000 plus yearly costs of $1500 for years 2 and 3. Compared to the ROI when no discounting is applied, the ROI when discounting by 3% for just 2 years is noticeably different [9]:

- Current year benefit = $2500
- Next year benefit = $2500 × (1 − 0.03) = $2425
- Following year benefit = $2500 × (1 − 0.03)^2 = $2352

The present value for the first 3 years of benefits = $2500 + $2425 + $2352 = $7277, which is less than 3 × $2500 = $7500, and allows for a more reasonable comparison to the investment that is necessary in the current year to achieve those benefits.

If there are ongoing costs in future years, those would be discounted in the same way. So, to extend this example, if the intervention involved an initial investment of $4000 and estimated ongoing costs of $1500 in each of the next two years, the present value for the first three years of costs would be:

$$\text{PV of costs} = \$4000 + \$1500 \times (1 - 0.03) + \$1500 \times (1 - 0.03)^2$$

Which equals $4000 + $1455 + $1411 = $6866, which is less than the raw amount of $7000.

Even though in this example we are discounting both costs and benefits, the results will produce different values for the ROI than when using the raw values. To see this, we can calculate the ROI each way:

$$\text{ROI using raw values} = (\$7500 - \$7000) / \$7000 \times 100\% = 5.98\%$$

$$\text{ROI using discounted values} = (\$7277 - \$6866) / \$6866 \times 100\% = 7.14\%$$

Therefore, while discounting itself is not complicated, be aware of the effect it can have on calculated metrics and also consider how the pattern and rate of costs and benefits affect the results.

6.2.4.2   Risk Adjustment

Risk adjustment is relevant for value-based payment policies through the role it plays in comparing quality or in the bundled payment that providers and facilities receive to care for certain types of patients. In general, risk adjustment is a statistical process that attempts to consider and incorporate characteristics of the entities being compared (e.g., hospitals, physicians, etc.) and/or characteristics of the patients they treat when comparing quality or determining payment.

Racial disparities exist in disease risk and prevalence, and social determinants of health play a significant role in maintaining health and treating illness. Therefore, a hospital that treats a racially and socioeconomically diverse population faces different challenges than one that treats a more homogenous population. Also, different hospitals have different levels of financial resources, equipment, and access to specialty care. Together, this suggests that treating the same condition may require very different costs and resources by these different hospitals and that patient outcomes may also differ even if the quality of care provided by the same hospitals is essentially equal.

How risk adjustment is employed is beyond the scope of this book. But, know that it attempts to account for these differences through the measurement of available patient and facility (or provider) information and the application of statistical models. And, while it may not be important to understand the details of how this process works, it is crucial to understand the strengths and weaknesses of risk adjustment.

The ability of risk adjustment to account for differences in patient populations and facility characteristics depends on the information used to risk adjust. First, these models can only risk adjust for factors that can be and are measured. Therefore, any unmeasured factors regarding these populations that affect health status or outcomes will not be accounted for in the risk adjustment model. (Common unmeasured factors could include level of trust of health care or authority in general, opinion about the effectiveness of medical treatment, willingness and ability to adhere to treatment, etc.) Further, even for measured factors, the quality of the data used to measure those factors will influence how well the risk adjustment performs. For example, if the only measurement of social determinants of health available to statisticians is, say, a county-level measure of average annual income, that may not fully capture the differences in social determinants between populations.

As with any method that involves the specification and development of a statistical model, debate will ensue about the extent to which risk adjustment accounts for true differences and how adequately it levels the playing field. Leveraging data and statistical models inherently introduces variability and potentially bias, which should also be considered. In general, while risk adjustment often plays an important role in value-based care, you should understand its role as a tool to help inform specific decisions.

6.3   Factors That Influence Health and Outcomes

When we attempt to assess value, we are often interested in patient outcomes and overall health as desired benefits to be weighed against some cost or investment. However, we must acknowledge the multiple factors that can impact the level of health and the frequency and severity of health outcomes.

Most often, we think about the role of healthcare providers or the healthcare delivery system as it relates to either promoting health or treating illness. Clearly, the choices made and the activities pursued by those treating patients impact the health and outcomes of patients. Therefore, we can assess value by examining those choices and activities. Additionally, patient behavior and decisions also play a role. Patients make choices about diet, exercise, lifestyle, when to seek care, and to what extent to follow treatment regimens (like adhering to medication). Many choices patients make are beyond the control of clinicians, and the reasons behind patient behavior are complex and multifaceted; and, some are intentional while others are unintentional (e.g., accidentally taking the wrong dose of a medication, missing a scheduled appointment due to unexpected circumstances, etc.). Therefore, interventions that positively affect patient behavior also have value to the extent that those changes improve health, outcomes, or the patient experience.

However, wider issues are at play, too. In recent years, researchers and policy makers have recognized the significant role social determinants of health play in patient care, in terms of access to care and outcomes. These determinants, like access to transportation, computer and/or Wi-Fi access, housing, food security, employment, and education influence patients' ability to access care, learn about care options, or connect with providers or social service people who may assist them.

Additionally, cultural and social paradigms impact health and outcomes, such as language barriers or inherent distrust of authority, science, or the government, all of which can influence choices patients make. Unequal care delivery or access by gender, race, and sexual orientation have all been demonstrated by various research studies over the years and cannot be discounted when considering the value of care and improvements to that care.

6.4   Summary

The tools commonly used to assess value of health and health care are numerous. Each requires certain assumptions and has advantages and disadvantages. At their core, these tools compare costs to benefits, monetary or otherwise, using various techniques and metrics. However, in each case, the issue of consistently defining value remains, as does the need to clarify from whose perspective value is viewed. As with any analytic methods, the appropriate use of these tools and the inferences drawn from them require careful consideration and the appropriate framework if they are to be applied effectively. Numerical techniques like discounting and risk adjustment are common and can help assessors make more meaningful comparisons, but they have limitations and neither is a panacea for addressing inherent differences in patients, providers, or systems.

References

1. Card WI, Mooney GH (1977) What is the monetary value of a human life? Br Med J 2(6103):1627–1629. https://doi.org/10.1136/bmj.2.6103.1627
2. Landefeld JS, Seskin EP (1982) The economic value of life: linking theory to practice. Am J Public Health 72(6):555–566. https://doi.org/10.2105/ajph.72.6.555
3. Kay TL (1990) Volume and intensity of medicare physicians' services: an overview. Health Care Financ Rev 11(4):133–146
4. Orkin FK (1993) Moving toward value-based anesthesia care. J Clin Anesth 5(2):91–98. https://doi.org/10.1016/0952-8180(93)90133-y
5. Porter ME (2010) What is value in health care? N Engl J Med 363(26):2477–2481. https://doi.org/10.1056/NEJMp1011024
6. Seixas BV, Dionne F, Conte T, Mitton C (2019) Assessing value in health care: using an interpretive classification system to understand existing practices based on a systematic review. BMC Health Serv Res 19(1):560. https://doi.org/10.1186/s12913-019-4405-6
7. Solid CA (2020) Return on investment for healthcare quality improvement. Springer Nature, Cham
8. Bentley TGK, Cohen JT, Elkin EB, Huynh J, Mukherjea A, Neville TH, Mei M, Copher R, Knoth R, Popescu I, Lee J, Zambrano JM, Broder MS (2017) Validity and reliability of value assessment frameworks for new cancer drugs. Value Health 20(2):200–205. https://doi.org/10.1016/j.jval.2016.12.011
9. Solid CA (2020) Costs and benefits. In: Return on investment for healthcare quality improvement. Springer, Cham. https://doi.org/10.1007/978-3-030-46478-3_4

Part III
Practical and Human Considerations: A Discussion of the Real-World Motivations and Requirements That Should Be Contemplated When Exploring Value

Chapter 7
Practical and Human Considerations

7.1 Perspectives

As mentioned previously, it is impossible to define value without specifying from whose perspective it is being viewed. Even though most would agree that reducing unnecessary hospitalizations has value, the nature and amount of that value are different for payers, patients, and society as a whole. There may be perspectives for whom it has very little value, like hospitals. While those caring for patients have an ethical and moral motivation to keep people healthy, health care is a business and reducing hospitalizations means less revenue for hospitals.

While the main perspectives are the ones I have listed previously, I will enumerate them here so that we can refer to them during the rest of the chapter as we explore various motivations, roles, and responsibilities related to health, health care, and assessing value. The primary perspectives often considered in value assessments include:

Patients. An argument can be made that when it comes to the value of health care, the patient perspective is the most important. Ultimately, the healthcare system exists to provide care to individuals who become ill or injured; and if our goal is to create "high-value" care, then viewing value through the eyes of the patient seems obvious. Benefits for this group include better health outcomes, better experiences, improved quality of life, more information, emotional and mental well-being, lower costs, less risk, more hope, and so on. Most of the time, costs will be limited to out-of-pocket expenses and/or time (which also may include lost wages from missed work). We may also consider what value is provided for the patient's family and/or informal caregivers. Benefits to patients (e.g., better experiences, lower costs, better outcomes) will typically also be benefits to caregivers, although their magnitude and/or how they are quantified may differ. Finally, it is worth noting that patients may often be underinformed or misinformed about the big picture and therefore (reasonably) only focused on their own experience. Value from their perspective then may be based on what they want instead of what would result in the best outcome for them. This also touches on topics related to human behavior and decision-making—and the inherent biases that can influence behavior and decisions, which we will soon explore more deeply.

Providers. This general category is meant to capture any and all entities that may deliver care and/or promote health to patients. Included are individual clinicians or groups of individuals within a hospital, clinic, or health system, or within larger aggregations of multiple entities. Community-based organizations (CBOs), social services, and other privately or publicly funded programs also fall into this category. While the structure and operation of CBOs, social services, and other programs may differ significantly from those of other providers, these entities still meet the definition of delivering care or promoting health; so for the purposes of assessing value, they are grouped with other providers. However, it would be uncommon to lump CBOs in with a hospital for a specific value assessment because it is likely that both providers would experience value very differently. For providers, value may stem from the care they provide (through wages or fees earned), the way they provide it (by efficient and/or expedient means), or the environment within which they provide it (through job satisfaction, autonomy, etc.). Like patients, costs for patients will typically involve investments of money and/or time.

Clinicians. Often, clinicians are included in the provider perspective, but not always. Sometimes, the clinician perspective is of direct interest in assessing value. For example, physician burnout is a serious problem in health care. Reducing this burnout has value from a provider perspective more generally by avoiding the cost of staff turnover, reducing the risk of errors and associated litigation that may stem from burnout, and so on. But, there is also value from a clinician perspective of improving clinician mental and emotional well-being. Depending on the motivation and goal of the intervention, we may want to separate this value from whatever financial value the facility or health system experiences. In other situations, the value from the clinician perspective may be slightly different from that of administrators or others typically grouped in the provider perspective. In those situations, it is prudent to define the clinician perspective separately.

Payers. Any group or entity that pays for care, either directly or through a reimbursement arrangement, can be considered a payer. The most common payers are insurance companies or health plans and government payers of Medicare and Medicaid. At times, it may be difficult to know where to draw the line between providers and payers. For example, hospitals incur costs to treat patients, but are not always fully reimbursed for those costs (particularly when treating Medicare/Medicaid patients). So, outside of any amount they can collect from another payer or the patient themselves, the hospital ends up absorbing and in a sense "paying" for a portion of the care. In most circumstances, the definitions of these categories do not matter much, but considering certain details regarding the differences between them for a given situation may. For example, if you were pitching a new process or service to a hospital by demonstrating its potential value to them, you may need to consider more than their costs and benefits associated with care delivery. You may also need to factor in their case mix or the target population since reimbursement can vary for different populations receiving the same care. Whether this reflects their mixed role as a provider/payer or whether it is just classified as a cost to them as a provider likely makes no difference as long as it is accounted for somewhere in your assessment. In general, benefits and costs from the payer perspective focus on the amount paid out to providers and/or patients.

Third-Party Healthcare Organization (TPHO). This group includes organizations that "equip" providers and patients with the tools and/or processes that help treat disease, promote health, and run the business of healthcare delivery. These are software companies, electronic health record vendors, medical device and digital health companies, suppliers of durable medical equipment, and so on. These are most often private companies, so that benefits often reflect sales, market share, guaranteed contracts, and so on. In some circumstances, the solutions TPHOs offer may be aimed directly at patients, while other times they aim for providers and/or payers to buy their produce or device. For this perspective, in particular, the intended audience can play a large role in determining how best to assess value. In some cases, TPHOs may be interested in demonstrating value to other TPHOs—specifically those they would like to partner with or be acquired by. That may involve different or additional sources of value that would be of interest to an acquiring organization (like increasing market share, keeping up with competition, etc.) but may not be of interest to a provider or payer.

Society. A societal perspective can take several forms. Some would suggest that components of patient well-being and family burden are part of a societal perspective. Most often, however, societal benefits reflect improvements in aggregate output, productivity, and health. Societal benefits also include reductions in absenteeism and presenteeism, increases to national measures of output like GDP, and health indicators like population disease prevalence/burden, or rates of major life events like births, deaths, infant mortality, and so on. In some ways, societal benefits are often a catchall for benefits that are not specific to any other perspective. Societal costs may involve government spending, taxes, and investments by public entities.

7.2 Motivations and Goals

Different perspectives will often have different experiences of value from the same activities, processes, or policies. Similarly, the motivations and desired outcomes may also differ by perspective. Obviously, patients are motivated to achieve high levels of health and well-being while reducing their costs in the form of money and time. A difficulty of population health is that despite these clear goals, patients often do not behave or make choices that are congruent with these outcomes. That is, patients often make poor choices regarding diet, exercise, substance use, smoking, and so on. Additionally, they have little to no imposed motivation to help limit payer costs. Regardless of the roles moral hazard, price insensitivity, and asymmetric information play, the practical reality is that patients often do not know what care costs or what payers ultimately pay for care; this makes it difficult to make choices consistent with limiting overall healthcare spending.

Payers, on the other hand, are motivated to limit their overall costs but also to promote population health and improve care quality. Therefore, they want to incentivize patients to utilize low-cost preventive care and make behavior choices that are consistent with high levels of population health (e.g., offering a premium discount for those who visit a gym a certain number of times per month). Payers also want to reward providers who deliver care that results in good patient outcomes and avoids excess utilization, errors, or adverse events. Once those providers have been identified, payers then want to direct patients to seek care from them in the form of preferred provider networks or "centers of excellence." Payers understand that patients are motivated, in part, by their desire to limit their out-of-pocket costs; so without other ways to compare providers, patients may likely select those for whom they have lower copays or deductibles (i.e., those in the preferred network).

The primary goal for providers involved in care delivery (one would hope) is to deliver the best care possible for their patients and make decisions that are in the patients' best interests. At the same time, providers understand that healthcare delivery is a business, and they must also make decisions that are consistent with their continued ability to stay open and afford to offer care. Additionally, providers understand the role quality monitoring and regulatory bodies play and are motivated to select actions that meet clinical guidelines and promote high performance on one or more quality measures. Some argue that these competing priorities put providers in an unfair position where they may have to make decisions that are inconsistent with the best possible care for their patients. Additionally, there is concern that monitoring some types of care delivery processes or outcomes may encourage providers to avoid treating risky patients or refuse to offer certain types of treatment. Other types of providers, like CBOs, trade groups, patient-advocacy groups, and such, are typically motivated by a mission centered around the patients or clinicians they represent.

Private, for-profit TPHOs (often device, med-tech, and digital health companies) have business-related goals in terms of revenues and profits, but most understand that this comes from successfully addressing a gap in the current care delivery process or developing a solution to a previously unsolved problem in patient care or population health. That is, they are motivated to "do well" financially but also by a desire to improve care delivery or efficiency in some way that ultimately benefits any or all of patients, providers, payers, and society.

Most often, society's motivation is considered to be to improve the overall welfare of the population as a whole—sometimes interpreted as "the most benefit for the most people," but there may be instances where welfare improvement is more nuanced than that. For our purposes, we can consider the societal motivation as generally seeking out the "good" or "better" result in a way that the other perspectives may not cover (Table 7.1).

Table 7.1 Motivations and goals related to health and health care

Perspective	Motivations and goals
Patients	• Achieve and maintain good health • Reduce cost (money and time)
Providers/ clinicians	• Deliver high-quality care • Act in their patients' best interests • Maintain financial viability • Meet clinical guidelines and regulations
Payers	• Limit costs • Promote population health (e.g., incentivize low-cost preventive health, encourage healthy behaviors and choices) • Improve care quality • Reward well-performing providers
TPHOs	• Increase revenues and profits • Successfully address gap in care, improve efficiency, enhance patient experience, or improve patient outcomes
Society	• Improve overall welfare of the population

7.3   Roles, Responsibilities, and Expectations

In addition to differences in motivations and goals, those from different perspectives also have different roles and responsibilities in providing high-quality care and promoting population health. We rarely discuss the expectations placed on different parties, even if they are universally accepted or assumed. But it is instructive to examine each perspective's roles, responsibilities, and expectations because they will play a role as we determine how to assess the value of different policies, decisions, behaviors, activities, and interventions.

Perhaps clinicians (and to some extent providers, more generally) have the clearest set of roles, responsibilities, and expectations placed on them. Their roles and responsibilities track closely with their motivations and goals: To serve in the best interest of their patients (especially in a "credence good" situation where patients largely cannot evaluate their own care options and the costs and benefits of each) and provide high-quality care while minimizing waste and unnecessary utilization.

More recently, there exists an expectation that providers should take more of a role in care coordination and population health and even serve as advocates for their patients if necessary. This expectation is imposed by policy makers, patients, and payers, but also by some providers themselves. This shifting expectation can cause difficulty given that historically providers have been responsible for episodes of care but not ongoing care outside of a specific setting. Some expectation of patient and family education and support also exists as well as promoting patient empowerment or patient activation, as described previously. Finally, many clinicians serve in more academic roles: Teaching and mentoring young clinicians, performing research, helping shape clinical guidelines, championing quality improvement initiatives, fostering an inclusive culture, and so on.

Patient roles and responsibilities have also shifted over the last few decades. By their own choice, patients have wanted to become more educated about their health and care choices and to participate in the care that is selected and administered (often referred to as "shared decision-making"). However, rarely is a specific expectation formally placed on a patient. One might *assume* that patients can be expected to adhere to their treatment regimen, follow clinical recommendations, and make healthy choices regarding their lifestyle and condition-specific requirements (e.g., dietary restrictions for certain medications). But when it comes to assessing the quality of care and espousing methods to improve care, typically the providers' actions and choices receive the focus. If patients are included, it is usually to provide more education or incentive to make good choices.

In short, a payer's role is to pay for care delivered. However, payers also have a role in negotiating prices of care services and resources, rooting out fraud and abuse, and determining what care options to offer members. Whether they have a responsibility to encourage high-quality care is debatable: Some would argue that their financial incentive to promote care quality and population health is a function of the system, not a result of the mission of the individual payer organizations. Unfortunately, many patients have expectations of payers that are adversarial in nature: That is, they expect the payer to "try to get out of paying" for some care the patient (and perhaps provider) believes is valid and justified. This relationship is unfortunate given that payers and patients have shared goals of high levels of population health, low costs, and high-quality care. This adversarial relationship can also complicate attempts to improve the value of care, although when assessing value the payer and patient perspectives are often aligned when identifying and quantifying benefits.

The role played by TPHOs is ultimately one of support or assistance. While they are motivated to create useful devices or technology from a business perspective, they serve that motivation by identifying inefficiencies or gaps in care and developing innovative solutions that can help providers deliver better care, faster, to more patients and/or for less money (i.e., more efficiently). In terms of responsibilities and expectations, other than to assume they will operate ethically and follow scientifically rigorous methods to develop and promote their healthcare solution not much else may be expected of them.

Society's role is often manifested through government policy or action. That is, most assume that government's role is to help encourage (if not ensure) equity when it comes to access, quality, and safety of care available and delivered to individuals, regardless of their characteristics or financial means. This means enacting and enforcing regulations, investigating and punishing fraud and abuse, offering assistance and education to the general public about health and safety, and providing oversight to treatment and therapy development and delivery. Most would say that society has a duty to help fund innovation, research, and improvements in care delivery. A societal perspective will often involve a balance of opposing forces. The goal of improving the population's health and welfare has to be balanced with the realities of limitations in cost and resources. And viewpoints differ regarding the level of involvement society (i.e., government) should have regarding oversight, mandates, and enforcement (Table 7.2).

Table 7.2 Roles, responsibilities, and expectations related to health and health care

Perspective	Motivations and goals
Patients	• Participate and take ownership of their health (adhere to treatment, make reasonable choices, participate in shared decision-making, etc.)
Providers/ Clinicians	• Deliver high-quality care • Act in their patients' best interests • Maintain financial viability • Serve as an advocate for their patients • Help coordinate patient care • Promote population health • Provide education to patients and families • Empower patients and include them in clinical decisions • Teach and mentor young clinicians, perform research, improve care quality, foster an inclusive facility culture, etc.
Payers	• Pay for care • Root out fraud and abuse of billing • Determine covered benefits
TPHOs	• Support and assist patients and providers through products, services, and innovation • Operate ethically and be scientifically rigorous
Society	• Promote/ensure equity • Enforce regulations • Investigate and punish fraud and abuse • Offer assistance and education to the public about health and safety • Provide oversight • Fund research and quality improvement

7.4   Social, Political, and Cultural Factors

We cannot consider human factors within any system without acknowledging the influence of social, political, and cultural forces on behavior, choices, and preferences. We would be naive to believe that if faced with the same decision and offered the same information that all individuals would make the same choice.

Therefore, when we consider the associated value of differing care quality, the impact of a particular device or solution, or look to incentivize specific behavior, we must think about the social, political, and cultural environment within which individual patients and providers reside.

We have discussed the model of healthcare delivery systems as complex adaptive systems or networks in a previous chapter (and will return to it in the next chapter), but we must also recognize and acknowledge that communities, social circles, and family units are also complex systems that impose their own influence on members' choices and behaviors.

Some examples of how social, political, or cultural factors include:

- The hierarchy of family and community members, including gender roles
- The role of religion or spiritual beliefs

- Opinions regarding death and the process of dying
- Faith in alternative medicines versus traditional medicine (including medications)
- Allegiance to political parties or politicians and their corresponding beliefs
- Generational norms (e.g., the appropriateness of questioning authority, desire to engage and take ownership for one's own health, the use of technology, expectations for communication)

This list is not exhaustive but illustrates the variety of factors that can potentially impact the timing and type of care sought out as well as the way and extent to which patients engage in their own care journey.

7.5 Behavioral Economics

The ability to quantify value to the extent that allows for decision-making assumes that we have an accurate impression of how the intervention or healthcare solution was or will be implemented and incorporated into everyday practice. Our understanding of care delivery across the various settings of care has evolved over time. What was once considered largely an aggregation of separate but related siloes of expertise, stratified by organ system or disease type, is now acknowledged to be a unique but interconnected network of semiautonomous individuals who can achieve more together than any one of them can on their own.

However, at the core of care delivery, quality improvement, technical innovation, and health management are individuals subject to human fallacies, assumptions, and biases. While an understanding of behavioral economics may not alter how we calculate the monetary benefit associated with a particular intervention, it will certainly provide a window into the process of quality improvement and implementation that can allow for a more thorough assessment of not only costs and benefits but of the drivers of those components within the complex adaptive system.

7.5.1 Complex Adaptive System (Redux)

The behavior of individuals working within a care delivery system cannot be separated from the system itself. That is, the representation of a hospital or health system as a complex adaptive system (CAS) acknowledges that while individual members are unique and autonomous, their choices and behaviors will be influenced by multiple components of their particular CAS, including:

- Interactions with colleagues and patients
- Physical environment
- Social and cultural environment
- Internal organizational forces

- External social, professional, and regulatory forces
- Previous experiences, clinical knowledge, beliefs, and opinions

It is perhaps no surprise then that the same patient presenting with the same symptoms may receive very different care depending on where they go or who they see. Even if ultimately the same diagnosis and treatment would be eventually provided, the process to get there may differ.

It should also be clear then that the ability of the CAS to adapt (to, say, a new process or the implementation of a quality improvement initiative) is also a function of those multiple components. This has important implications for not only those seeking to improve the quality or efficiency of care but also for those trying to assess what value is *possible* to capture and how best to explore it.

One of the most important implications of a complex adaptive system is the phenomenon of *emergence* that they often exhibit [1, 2]. In technical terms, emergence is when individual components of a CAS come together to produce new or unpredictable characteristics or behaviors—those that would not have been predicted if only the individual members had been studied. In layperson's terms, this is the sentiment of "the whole is greater than the sum of its parts." This suggests that to only assess the value of a single member or component of a CAS may misrepresent the overall value the system produces if one were to try to generalize it. In other words, just because a new care pathway or electronic decision tool did not produce the desired efficiency for an individual clinician or even department does not mean that the (lack of) value demonstrated by use of that new pathway or decision tool can be extrapolated to the entire organization.

Also of interest as it relates to the value of implemented changes or new innovations is how information and practices are diffused across the network. When it comes to the diffusion of innovation, no model is more often referenced than that of Everett M. Rogers, who first published his theories in the 1960s and developed the now-famous bell curve of diffusion that labeled individuals as "innovators," "early adopters," "early majority," "late majority," or "laggards," depending on where they fell on the distribution of the time it took to adopt a new process. Unfortunately, many have applied this model to the healthcare system even though much of the underlying assumptions do not apply in a healthcare setting. For example, Rogers's work relates to optional innovation decisions, while often healthcare settings incorporate mandated policy changes. Additionally, the nature of a CAS would typically promote a much faster rate of diffusion of an innovation throughout the organization than would be true in Rogers's model [3]. Rogers himself has acknowledged that how interconnected the network within an organization is and the presence of influential members (e.g., like hospital leadership) would affect the rate of diffusion [4].

The takeaway is that if healthcare delivery systems can be considered to function as CASs, then much of the prevailing theory regarding how to implement change (and therefore the ability to capture potential value that comes from those changes) needs to be reconsidered. The behavior of the network is a function of the nature of individuals' interactions and connections. It is also a function of their humanness, which we now explore further.

7.5.2 System Thinking and Cognitive Biases

One of the basic tenets of much of economic theory predicting individual decisions and behavior is that those within the economic model are "rational." For example, the assumption is that if faced with two prices for the same good, all individuals would select the cheaper one, every time. In economic terms, this assumption involves "maximizing the consumer's utility function" or making decisions that are in their best interest. This lays the foundation for theories of supply, demand, and prices, and seems reasonable in the hypothetical examples of a typical Econ 101 class; but it imposes certain restrictions and limits the applicability of some results to real situations.

Studies of human behavior, in fact, paint a far more complex picture. Countless examples exist of individuals consistently making what one would consider an irrational choice, such as sticking with a current insurance plan even if a less expensive or more comprehensive plan becomes available or selecting a type of treatment against the advice of a physician simply because a trusted friend suggested they try it. Nobel Prize winner Herbert Simon used the term "bounded rationality" to represent the reality that limitations in knowledge, cognitive capacity, attention, time, and so on, impede an individual's ability to make choices [5]. As a result, individuals may not always do the hard work of seeking out the "optimal" solution, instead settling for one that is "good enough."

Work by Amos Tversky and Daniel Kahneman (another Nobel winner) demonstrates that when individuals are faced with limitations in time or information they fall back on what Tversky and Kahneman referred to as "heuristics" to make decisions. Heuristics are like shortcuts or rules of thumb that individuals use to make decisions when information or time is limited or incomplete—the exact scenario Simon's definition of bounded rationality describes. Kahneman suggests that individuals employ two cognitive systems. One is a fast, automated, and intuitive system (he named it simply "System 1") that requires little cognitive effort and allows for quick reactions. The other ("System 2") is deliberate and contemplative and as a result is slow and resource intensive [6]. Therefore, when information, time, or cognitive resources are scarce, one may unknowingly default to System 1 thinking, relying on heuristics that may introduce bias into the decision-making process.

More than a 100 heuristics have been identified [7], but one of the original ones Tversky and Kahneman identified—and one that illustrates how heuristics are used and may introduce bias—is the "availability" heuristic. This describes the tendency for individuals to unconsciously consider examples that quickly come to mind (i.e., that are easily "available") when evaluating a situation or selecting a behavior. Frequently, this heuristic manifests when evaluating the potential consequences of actions: Reading about increased crime in your area may cause you to overestimate the likelihood that your car will get broken into if you leave it parked on the street overnight; seeing social media posts about rare medication side effects may result in you inflating your own risk of a side effect if you were to be prescribed that medication. Clinicians, too, can be influenced by the availability heuristic. When diagnosing a patient, they may be influenced (even if only slightly) by a recent uptick in a particular disease that shares symptoms with those seen in the presenting patient. Or in recommending a treatment, they may be more influenced by their own recent experiences with patients in a similar situation than by aggregated scientific evidence regarding the optimal treatment.

While this description of human cognition has implications for how to best encourage certain behaviors and decisions during the care delivery process, it also has importance for the interpretation and dissemination of value assessments. Because value assessments are typically performed to make informed decisions about what course of action to take, those presenting the results need to be aware of the potential biases of those receiving the results.

7.6   Biases Impacting the Design and Interpretation of Value Assessments

Despite the negative connotation of its name, cognitive bias is not always bad, especially if it is understood and used to encourage beneficial behavior or efficient choices. Implementation science has begun to leverage commonly accepted heuristics to redesign processes, develop interventions, or adjust the physical environment to help foster and encourage specific behaviors or activities. Effective interventions may incorporate different "nudges," such as showing physicians their antibiotic prescription frequency compared to peers to leverage the social norm heuristic or presenting choices in a certain order to leverage the framing and/or ordering effect. Using nudges or a series of nudges (a "choice architecture") to encourage behavior can be a powerful tool.

However, cognitive biases can potentially impact our ability to accurately predict or measure value, and it behooves those seeking to assess value to identify the risk of certain biases within their own examination. The following list is by no means exhaustive, but it illustrates how we might proceed to think about biases and mitigate their influence.

7.6.1   Biases That Can Influence Value Measurement

Certain biases have the largest influence on our ability to accurately identify, measure, or quantify impact or change (and therefore value). Some examples include:

- **The observer effect (or "Hawthorne effect")** suggests that clinicians and patients tend to behave differently when they know they're being observed. This can be especially complicating when establishing a baseline that you hope to improve upon. Whether that baseline is adherence to a particular therapy, remembering to advise patients about a specific treatment, or some other process or event, those being observed may be more aware of the issue and end up performing better than they would have if they were not observed or did not realize their performance was being monitored. The observer effect reduces the potential for improvement and can reduce the quantifiable value from realizing an improvement.

- **Attribution error** is the tendency to overestimate the impact of personal attributes on outcomes and underestimate how much situational factors play a role [8]. For example, when attributing medical errors, one tends to focus on characteristics of the clinician or clinicians involved and what is true about them, as opposed to the particulars of the situation in which they made the error. This may lead to inaccurate assumptions about how to reduce errors or how best to measure and evaluate how effective a particular intervention or solution is toward that goal.
- **Optimism bias** typically refers to our own tendency to underestimate the likelihood of experiencing a negative event and to overestimate the likelihood of experiencing a positive event; but it can also apply to other situations. In one example, researchers observed that clinicians overestimated their own patients' medication adherence compared to patients in general [9]. This may result in assumptions that are overly optimistic in terms of the ability of an intervention or solution to improve patient outcomes or influence behavior, which may lead to overestimating potential benefits or underestimating costs used to calculate the associated value.

7.6.2 Biases That Can Influence Value Interpretation

In addition to biases that impact our ability to assess value, some biases affect our ability to interpret the results objectively and can make communicating results to audiences more challenging.

- **Hindsight bias** is broadly defined as the tendency to overestimate the extent to which a past event could or should have been predicted or expected. Within health care, this often manifests in retrospective evaluations of care quality once outcomes are known. Researchers in the United Kingdom observed significant hindsight bias in the review of similar case "vignettes." Their analysis revealed that in some instances, those reviewing the cases "exhibited significantly more critical assessments of the same antecedent care when the patient had died" than when the patient survived [10]. The authors go on to conclude that this could have positive and negative consequences depending on the situation and point of view; but for our purposes, it simply signals the potential for bias in interpreting the value of care delivered.
- **The sunk cost bias and the IKEA effect** both relate to the influence personal connections to systems or processes can have on the value assigned to them. This

can manifest in a number of ways. Perhaps a patient or provider continues to pursue an ineffective course of treatment simply because time and resources have already been invested in it. If presenting results to a board tasked with whether to scrap a certain program or continue to offer it, any person or group who helped develop or implement the program will likely have a higher opinion of it because they were involved in its creation.

- **The Pelzman effect** refers to how individuals adjust or "compensate" behavior when safety measures are put into place [11]. The classic example is the idea that once seatbelts were mandated, drivers became slightly less cautious. In health care, incorporating technology that reduces the likelihood of a medical error or adverse event may make clinicians or patients less careful or vigilant about those errors. This may mean that expected improvements or reductions in these errors or events attributed to that technology may be dampened slightly by the change in behavior of those involved.

Obviously, these are just a few examples, but they demonstrate the importance of understanding behavioral economic concepts and seeking out information regarding specific heuristics and biases that may impact a specific value assessment. Even if there are no steps to take to mitigate the potential effects, acknowledging and considering the impacts can help solidify the business case you are trying to make with your value assessment by demonstrating the thoroughness of your examination.

7.7 Summary

We often omit practical and human considerations from discussions of value assessments, which tend to focus on technical aspects of different methodologies. However, the complexity of human nature, cognitive biases, sociocultural dynamics of care teams, and other components all influence the decisions and behaviors involved in health promotion and treatment of disease. Therefore, the myriad of practical and human components directly impact the value of any intervention, process, product, device, or solution attempting to improve care or promote health. Understanding some of the underlying theories that explain decision-making and behavioral choices is critical to understanding the value that results from such activities. With this final piece, we can begin to develop a framework for designing, performing, and interpreting value assessments.

References

1. Lambert P (2018) The ontological emergence of creativity
2. Lambert P (2018) The complex adaptive process of innovation diffusion
3. Lambert P (2018) Innovation diffusion: a complex adaptive process
4. Rogers EM (2003) Diffusion of innovations, 5th edn. Free Press, New York

5. Simon HA (1990) Bounded rationality. In: Eatwell J, Milgate M, Newman P (eds) Utility and probability. Palgrave Macmillan, London
6. Kahneman D (2011) Thinking, fast and slow. Farrar, Straus and Giroux, New York
7. Cognitive Bias Codex (2021). VisualCapitalist.com. https://www.visualcapitalist.com/wp-content/uploads/2017/09/cognitive-bias-infographic.html. Accessed 31 Aug 2021
8. Artino AR Jr, Durning SJ, Waechter DM, Leary KL, Gilliland WR (2012) Broadening our understanding of clinical quality: from attribution error to situated cognition. Clin Pharmacol Ther 91(2):167–169. https://doi.org/10.1038/clpt.2011.229
9. Clyne W, McLachlan S, Mshelia C, Jones P, De Geest S, Ruppar T, Siebens K, Dobbels F, Kardas P (2016) "My patients are better than yours": optimistic bias about patients' medication adherence by European health care professionals. Patient Prefer Adherence 10:1937–1944. https://doi.org/10.2147/ppa.s108827
10. Banham-Hall E, Stevens S (2019) Hindsight bias critically impacts on clinicians' assessment of care quality in retrospective case note review. Clin Med (Lond) 19(1):16–21. https://doi.org/10.7861/clinmedicine.19-1-16
11. Prasad V, Jena AB (2014) The Peltzman effect and compensatory markers in medicine. Healthcare 2(3):170–172. https://doi.org/10.1016/j.hjdsi.2014.05.002

Part IV
How to Design and Perform a Value Assessment

Chapter 8
The Value Assessment Framework

8.1 Overview

The framework presented in the following pages intends to offer guidance for how to plan, develop, and carry out value assessments of all types of interventions and solutions and then to communicate them to a specific audience. The primary components of the assessment framework will not surprise you. They are:

1. Define exactly what constitutes value for a given situation.
2. Determine the costs and benefits and the metrics used to compare them.
3. Interpret the results for the intended audience.

Within each primary component reside several key aspects to consider, definitions to establish, and assumptions to specify. The fact that you can apply the same framework to two very different situations to produce two very different methodologies is exactly the point: While the results may not be directly comparable because of the different situations, you can be confident that both contain an equal amount of rigor and robustness because they share a common process that provides the foundation upon which the results are built.

Correspondingly, when two similar situations use the same or similar methodology, comparison is more likely than it would have been if each had been independently developed without a standard framework. Therefore, using a common framework may homogenize value assessments of similar interventions or within similar settings or disease areas to the point where comparisons of value are reasonable. It may even allow for the establishment of consistent definitions for components of value or metrics in some situations. For example, imagine if all value assessments of efforts to reduce rehospitalizations reported a cost-per-hospitalization avoided in addition to any other metrics the assessor deemed informative. Given the wide variety in what hospitalizations cost payers and patients, a metric based solely on the avoided outcome and the investment required to achieve that outcome could be universally interpreted. Movement toward any degree of standardization would permit direct comparisons across interventions to improve decision-making and confidence regarding those decisions.

Ultimately, that is what this is all about: Assisting decision makers by equipping them with the most accurate, valid, and useful information regarding the value of individual activities or solutions. The usefulness of this framework depends on its ability to provide the guidance and structure needed to develop and carry out value assessments that result in that type of information.

In a general sense, this process endeavors to systematically describe for a particular audience:

1. "Here's what we believe constitutes value in this situation."
2. "Here's how we will measure, quantify, and evaluate that value."
3. "Here's what our findings mean."

Table 8.1 shows the value assessment framework components. The following pages include details of each step and specific suggestions for how to utilize this framework.

8.2 Motivating Examples

Let's consider two examples of completed value assessments to better illustrate the framework components. I draw these examples from real studies and projects I have either worked on or am familiar with. These examples will provide some consistency and a common thread to help you follow how the components of the value assessment build upon one another. Each will include information on (1) how value is defined, (2) what costs and benefits will be measured and what metrics will be used to reflect value, and (3) how the findings related to value will be interpreted and communicated.

8.2.1 Example 1: Reducing Central Line-Associated Bloodstream Infections (CLABSIs)

As a relatively straightforward example, consider a hospital department's attempts to reduce central line-associated bloodstream infections (CLABSIs) through implementing a "prevention bundle"—a series of practices that have been proven to reduce the likelihood of infections. Best practices for preventing CLABSIs include regularly changing tubing and dressing, ensuring sterile techniques with line placement, and maintaining basic hand hygiene.

The hospital department is motivated to reduce CLABSIs for multiple reasons. First, CLABSI reduction represents a quality measure they are evaluated on as part

Table 8.1 The value assessment framework components

Framework component	Description
Define value	
Perspective	Value to whom?
Scope	Specify details related to the timing, setting, intensity, population, and duration the assessment covers
Goal(s) or objective(s)	Clearly state the motivation, goals, purpose, or the decision the assessment will inform
Assumptions	Identify the assumptions used in the value assessment, and explicitly state them
Intended audience	Determine for whom you are performing the assessment
Identify costs, benefits, and metrics	
Cost sources and measurements	Identify the sources of the costs and benefits, determine the measurements and quantification of each cost and benefit, and establish the level of attribution they have to the intervention, product, service, or solution being assessed.
Benefit sources and measurements	
Appropriate metrics	Explore various metrics that may be useful; multiple metrics may be appropriate for the same assessment. Identify relevant comparisons or benchmarks if applicable
Interpret and communicate	
Explore all types of value	Value is more than financial return; be sure to explore nonmonetary costs and benefits and place the results in context
Inform, guide, and teach	A value assessment should do more than just restate what is already known
Merge practical and technical considerations	Combining technical results with practical realities can help make the assessment credible and compelling
Identify learnings and new insights	Describe anything that the value assessment unearthed that was new or previously unknown
Describe what's needed going forward	Value assessments should not be a one-time endeavor

of a value-based reimbursement structure, so improved performance would likely mean increased revenue. Second, because CLABSI rates are publicly reported, hospital administrators know that improvement may also increase their safety reputation. This would result in higher scores in patient satisfaction quality measures, which could also increase revenues from the same value-based reimbursement program and potentially improve their "brand" as a high-quality hospital. For the hospital's clinicians and administrators, a reduction in CLABSIs has measurable value in terms of an increased likelihood that patients may select their facility for elective procedures or preventive care. One of the hospital's goals is to demonstrate the value of the "prevention bundle" initiative to their board to justify the investment and garner the board's support for other initiatives they hope to pursue in the future.

While a full report of a completed value assessment can be lengthy and include numerous tables and graphs, the executive summary of the value assessment for the CLABSI reduction example could look something like the following:

Executive Summary of CLABSI Value Assessment

Value Defined

We sought to assess the of a quality improvement initiative to reduce CLABSIs among all patients admitted to our department between January and June of this year who required a central line. Our goal for this analysis is to determine, from the hospital's perspective, whether the internal costs incurred to implement a comprehensive "prevention bundle" produced a positive financial return. For this analysis, we will assume that 100% of the reduction in CLABSI rates was directly due to the intervention, but we are limiting the examination to reductions in CLABSIs, excluding any observed reductions in other infections or improvements in other safety measures during the 6-month period. We believe this will result in a conservative estimate of the potential financial return.

Costs, Benefits, and Metrics Identified

For this analysis, we consider costs from the hospital's perspective that are directly related to the planning, preparation, and implementation of the prevention bundle. Measured benefits include the estimated increase in reimbursement revenue from quality monitoring programs that use CLABSI as one of the criteria to determine reimbursement. Our results indicate that the ROI for this particular intervention is between 17 and 23%. This improvement in performance exceeds the returns realized from previous quality improvement initiatives implemented during the last 2 years.

Findings Interpreted and Communicated

Our interpretation of these results indicates that this was a prudent financial investment and that future initiatives of this type are likely to result in a positive ROI for the hospital. Additionally, we enumerate additional sources of value we believe resulted from this initiative, which we were unable to measure or quantify with specificity, including improvements in hospital brand and reputation, increased job satisfaction and engagement among staff, and the general learnings gained regarding the implementation of quality improvement in our facility. Specifically, we describe barriers and challenges faced and the executed solutions, and we have also included recommendations for future quality initiatives. We plan to monitor CLABSI rates and report on the sustainability of this initiative over the next 12 months, at which time we will recalculate the estimated financial return.

Note that in practice, much of what is included in the value definition as well as the sources of costs and benefits would be specified during the planning and development of the assessment; once completed, specific results would then be inserted and interpreted for the intended audience.

Table 8.2   The value framework applied to the CLABSI example

Framework component	CLABSI example
Define value	
Perspective	Provider
Scope	Patients with a central line placed during the 6-month observation period
Goal(s) or objective(s)	Demonstrate positive financial return
Assumptions	Reductions in CLABSI are 100% attributed to the intervention Any spillover effects on other safety improvements or infection reductions are excluded from the value calculation
Intended audience	The hospital board
Identify costs, benefits, and metrics	
Cost sources and measurements	Materials, training, and staff time
Benefit sources and measurements	Increased revenue from value-based reimbursement programs, improved brand or reputation
Appropriate metrics	ROI, benefit-to-cost ratio (BCR), payback period
Interpret and communicate	
Explore all types of value	Increased revenue, improvements in brand and reputation, patient health and well-being, increased facility knowledge regarding initiative implementation
Inform, guide, and teach	Gained knowledge regarding implementation, better understanding of how best to plan and carry out initiatives
Merge practical and technical considerations	Technical involves the prevention bundles and how they reduced CLABSIs; practical considerations include identified barriers and solutions to overcome barriers
Identify learnings and new insights	Challenges faced during implementation, identified solutions, learnings for the next initiative
Describe what's needed going forward	Continued updates on the sustainability and continued value aggregation

If we were to transfer the information from the hospital's narrative to the table that includes the framework components, it would look like Table 8.2.

8.2.2   Example 2: Increasing Coverage and Offerings for Mental and Behavioral Health

As another example, imagine that a private insurance company has determined that offering more coverage for mental and behavioral health services would produce a net positive financial return for their company, even if member premiums were not raised. Presumably, actuaries at the insurance company predict that by covering mental and behavioral health services more broadly, members who need such services would be more likely to use them, and that in turn would reduce the need for more serious and expensive care for conditions that can result from untreated mental or behavioral health needs. That is, the insurance company expects a net reduction in expenditures because any increase in spending for the now-covered mental and behavioral health services would be more than offset by the reduction in spending for the treatment of more serious conditions. Additionally, the company believes that offering this coverage represents an opportunity to attract new members and retain current members for longer if it can adequately communicate the value of this benefit to current and potential members.

Therefore, the insurance company seeks to illustrate, from a patient perspective, the value of the increased coverage of mental and behavioral health services. One of the company's goals is to create member-facing communication materials illustrating the value of their newly enhanced mental and behavioral health offerings, which would be shaped in part by a marketing and design team so that it would be likely to engage current or potential members. In summarizing the results of the assessment in preparation for the development of that member-facing document, brochure, or web content, that executive summary might look like this:

Executive Summary for the Increased Mental and Behavioral Health Coverage Value Assessment

Value Defined

This document contains the results of an assessment of the increased value that value plan members would experience as a result of the increased coverage for mental and behavioral health services. We attempted to quantify the yearly benefits from the member perspective, assuming that expected improvements in mental and behavioral-related outcomes over previous years' levels among our member population could be directly and 100% attributed to the additional coverage. Our goal is to attract and retain more plan members by clearly illustrating this value to current and potential members.

Costs, Benefits, and Metrics Identified

For this analysis, we do not assign any costs to members because the added benefits are not associated with an increase in premiums. We understand that potential members may incur costs if they decide to switch from a different plan to this one, but we are unable to estimate what those costs may be. We assume the main benefit sources to be lower out-of-pocket costs to plan members for mental and behavioral health services and the lower likelihood of adverse mental and behavioral health outcomes, which have implications for quality of life and health-related expenditures. We calculate estimated savings per member on an annual basis.

Findings Interpreted and Communicated

In addition to financial value, we describe the value members may receive from improved quality of life and increased peace of mind simply from knowing that the new services are available. We hope to inform current and potential members of the seriousness of mental and behavioral health and what new services are covered. We understand that from a practical stand-point, even when services are covered members may be reluctant to access them due to fear of stigma or for privacy concerns. Therefore, we include in our value assessment a section addressing real-world practices for accessing these services. Finally, we round out our assessment of the value of these added services by describing our plan to provide annual updates to members on how the new coverage benefits have affected patient well-being and we will re-evaluate coverage policies to ensure the highest possible value to members going forward.

As with the CLABSI example, we can pull information from this narrative to popu-late the table we originally created; this will allow us to see how the specific details from this example address the individual components (Table 8.3).

Equipped with these two examples, let us dive more deeply into the components of the framework and the individual aspects that make it up.

8.3   Step 1 of the Value Assessment Framework: Define Value

Given the subjective nature of the concept of value and the wide variability in value definitions that exist across the healthcare system, defining value for any given assessment is not easy. To ensure that we establish a thorough and complete defini-tion, we need to ask five questions when defining:

1. From whose perspective we are considering value—value to whom?
2. What is the scope of the value assessment in terms of time and reach?
3. What is (are) the value assessment's goal(s) or objective(s) (e.g., what decision(s) will it inform)?
4. What assumptions will be made in the value assessment?
5. Who is the intended audience for the value assessment?

Often, these components of the value definition will be considered simultane-ously or at least iteratively because each can determine or inform one or more of the others. However, the omission of any one of these five components may result in a deficiency in the value assessment and therefore the usefulness of the ultimate results. We will examine each of the five questions that help us determine what will constitute value.

Table 8.3 The value assessment framework applied to the insurance company example

Framework component	Insurance company example
Define value	
Perspective	Patient
Scope	All current and prospective members over the course of 1 year
Goal(s) or objective(s)	Attract and retain more plan members
Assumptions	Improvements in mental and behavioral health-related outcomes are 100% attributable to added coverage
Intended audience	Current and potential plan members
Identify costs, benefits, and metrics	
Cost sources and measurements	Unknown
Benefit sources and measurements	Lower out-of-pocket costs, less likelihood of the need for more intensive treatment, personal satisfaction with health plan
Appropriate metrics	Reduction in out-of-pocket costs, improved quality of life, and reduced work absenteeism for plan members
Interpret and communicate	
Explore all types of value	Improvements in quality of life, increased peace of mind
Inform, guide, and teach	A better understanding of what services are covered and what they can mean for individual members
Merge practical and technical considerations	Technical involves the specifics of the coverage; practical considerations include real-world use and implications of the benefits
Identify learnings and new insights	A better understanding of the role played by mental and behavioral health, and its value to members
Describe what's needed going forward	Annual updates on how the new coverage benefits have affected patient well-being

8.3.1   Question 1: From Whose Perspective Are We Considering Value—Value to Whom?

Specifying the perspective is critical for any value assessment. We cannot talk about value without getting specific about "value to whom."

To determine the perspective is to point the assessment in a particular direction that informs not only what costs and benefits we consider, but how we measure, quantify, and compare them. For example, if aiming to reduce adverse events like infections, the chosen perspective determines how the associated benefits will be identified and quantified. From a patient perspective, the benefits of fewer infections include better health and quality of life; for a payer, the benefits are the reductions in costs spent treating infections. Similarly, the efforts needed to avoid the event differ by perspective and involve different sets of costs. Identifying the perspective will also help clarify the relevant costs and benefits and the appropriate way to quantify them. In our CLABSI example, performing the assessment from the provider's perspective signals that it will include costs the hospital incurred to implement the initiative and benefits accrued as a result of reductions in CLABSIs.

The perspective is also frequently linked to the intended audience. Often, they are one and the same. For example, if you're trying to demonstrate the value of a medical device to a payer, you want to illustrate how the solution conveys savings realized through the costs and benefits for that payer. Here, the audience and perspective are the same. Now consider another example where the audience and perspective differ; let's say policy makers or governing bodies are the audience and they want to establish guidelines for care that maximize patient outcomes. In this case, we consider value from the patient's perspective, since an increase in value to patients is what would be used to determine the success of the initiative or guideline.

A statement indicating whose perspective the assessment is considering in your assessment is often the first indication to the audience of the goal of the assessment and signals much of what is to follow. If a payer or provider perspective is chosen, you might assume that the assessment intends to demonstrate cost savings or improved efficiencies; a patient perspective suggests that relevant benefits will involve life years or quality of life. The examples presented at the beginning of the chapter illustrate how naming a perspective helps signal the goal of the assessment: The CLABSI example's payer perspective signals the goal to demonstrate a financial return to the hospital, while the insurance company example's patient perspective suggests that the goal is to convince members (or potential members) of the value of the new coverage.

If we identify more than one perspective as relevant to the value assessment, we need additional detail regarding how the multiple perspectives will be handled. Will separate analyses be performed for each perspective? Or will all the perspectives be considered within the same analysis? If it is the latter, we need to be clear (either at the outset or later on when costs, benefits, and metrics are discussed) about how we will express, combine, or reconcile the individual values as they relate to each perspective. If payer and provider perspectives are both relevant, for example, how will reductions in utilization translate to costs and benefits for each? Less utilization reflects cost savings for payers but may be seen as a revenue loss for providers. Addressing this type of potential complexity or dual role of certain costs or benefits should be done up front.

Obviously, it is a lot easier to include multiple perspectives in an analysis when they experience the same or similar costs and benefits or when their interests align. For example, patient and societal perspectives can typically be combined or at least presented together in the same analysis because what is good for patients is often good for population health, productivity, or other outcomes thought of as societal benefits. Providers and payers, on the other hand, might be difficult to combine because revenue from care utilization is a benefit for providers but may reflect costs for payers. Both the CLABSI example and the insurance company example consider only a single perspective. In fact, they specifically identify the perspective they consider:

- CLABSI example: "Our goal from this analysis is to determine, from the hospital's perspective, whether the internal costs incurred to implement a comprehensive 'prevention bundle' produced a positive financial return."

- Insurance company example: "We attempted to quantify the yearly benefits from the member perspective…"

While they may acknowledge that multiple perspectives exist that may receive benefits (e.g., the CLABSI example could note the inherent value to patients of fewer infections), they are clear about what value is included in the results being presented.

8.3.2   Question 2: What Is the Scope of the Value Assessment in Terms of Time and Reach?

Defining the scope of a value assessment sets parameters for its breadth and depth by specifying details related to the timing, setting, intensity, and/or other aspects of the initiative whose value is being assessed. Defining the scope not only gives direction regarding what costs and benefits will be included, it also begins to indicate what comparisons might be appropriate as a result of the assessment or what decisions the assessment may inform. In short, the scope signals the objective for the assessment and for whom the assessment is for (i.e., the intended audience). When describing a value assessment, the perspective and scope are often stated alongside one another, as in "this analysis reflects perspectives of patients with diabetes aged sixty and older who are living at home and receiving no in-home care services."

Individual components of the scope of a value assessment may include one or more of the following:

1. The time period over which an initiative or change is assessed
2. The setting and/or population affected by the initiative or change

Time period. There may be a variety of stages of an intervention or implementation of a new process or device, but for a value assessment, specifying a time period indicates the period during which costs and benefits will be considered. This may be calendar-based, like a month, a quarter, or a year, or it may be based on the specifics of the solution being evaluated. For a process improvement intervention, the time period will likely begin at some point prior to the start of the intervention through its completion and perhaps into a follow-up or "sustainment" period. At times, the time period may be implied or mentioned indirectly, as opposed to specifically stated up front.

For example, if a digital health company wants to demonstrate the value of their solution through the reduction of an adverse event within a specific population, their assessment may use information from previously published studies for rates of that event or the percentage of patients who experience that event prior to when their solution is and is not used. More than likely, whether they realize it or not, when performing their calculations they are assuming a time period that corresponds to those used in the published rates or percentages they quote. That is, they may simply say, "with our solution, rates of the adverse event dropped from 17.8 per 100 patient months to 5.2, which equates to an expected reduction of roughly 6.5 events in our population of 250 patients per month." We are left to infer that they are assessing value either during a single month or will use that monthly rate to extrapolate to other time periods (such as 6 or 12 months). It is better to explicitly state the associated time period so that it is clear and no one is left to determine it on their own through studying the results.

The appropriate time frame for a value assessment will often depend on several things. In the CLABSI example, the length of the initiative and the amount of data available likely drove the determination of the appropriate time frame. However, those performing the assessment need to determine how much time before and after the implementation period to include. Costs may have been incurred as the department readied for the initial implementation, or there may be ongoing costs that remain after the official end of the initiative (Fig. 8.1).

There may be no right or wrong answer regarding the time frame, and it may even be something those performing the assessment adjust as they continue to develop the assessment. For the private insurance company, the chosen time frame may also have been driven by available data. Those performing the assessment had to think about what information they would use to demonstrate value to plan members. They needed to decide whether to present data on the average out-of-pocket expenditures for mental and behavioral services that are now fully covered or data on how utilizing such services can improve mental and emotional well-being, reduce work absenteeism, or reduce the need for more intense treatments. The insurance company's value assessors likely performed some preliminary research into what data or estimates were available to determine the appropriate time frame.

Setting and/or affected population. The setting may be geographic, such as a state or region; clinical, such as a hospital or clinic; or characteristic, such as urban/rural or academic/nonacademic. The affected population may be patients, but it may also be any of the other perspectives as well. For example, for an intervention intended to lower staff turnover, the affected population is the individual staff members even if the audience of the value capture is the facility administration. When the affected population is a group of patients, we need a level of specificity to focus the costs and benefits to the appropriate level of detail. For example, if a device company aims to improve medication adherence among community-dwelling adults

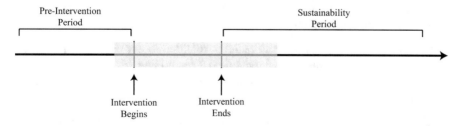

Fig. 8.1 Determining the time frame for the value assessment. If the gray bar represents the value assessment time frame, we need to decide how much time before and after the implementation of a change or intervention to include in the assessment

with high blood pressure, it is unlikely that *all* community-dwelling adults with high blood pressure would be the appropriate group for a value assessment of the device. If the device improves blood pressure control by improving medication adherence, then the device can only help a subset of those individuals—specifically those whose high blood pressure is caused by poor adherence. Individuals who are adherent to their antihypertensive medication but still have high blood pressure (i.e., treatment-resistant hypertensives) and those unable or unwilling to use a device due to cognitive impairment or other reasons will not be the affected population. A savvy audience (in this case, perhaps the creators and/or administrators of a health plan) will recognize the difference, and the device company will be better served to get specific about their affected population.

The patient populations and timings used in the CLABSI and insurance company examples illustrate the thought process involved in identifying what is appropriate. In the CLABSI example, the chosen population included patients treated in the department who have a central line inserted at some point during their stay since they are at risk of a CLABSI. However, it is not uncommon for the impact of a safety-improving initiative to spill over into other areas; and this department may have observed improvements in other safety metrics, such as reductions in other types of hospital-acquired infections because some of the best practices for preventing one kind of infection can help prevent other types of infections. Therefore, their value assessment could have included a larger patient population (i.e., all patients treated in the department) to allow for inclusion of the other benefits in the value calculation, assuming it is reasonable to attribute some or all the observed reduction in other infections to the CLABSI-focused activities.

Similarly, while the private insurance company's increased coverage of mental and behavioral health services may truly impact only those with mental or behavioral health needs, those designing the assessment need to consider whether the affected population should be limited to those individuals. Other individuals considering different insurance plans may value the increased coverage because they feel comforted that those services would be covered if they ever needed them or because they feel as though the increased covering reflects a certain characteristic about the plan that they appreciate. Perhaps some individuals gain a more favorable opinion about the insurance company because of the additional offerings, even if they were never to use them. In each example, different patient populations may require different assumptions, measurements, data, or metrics, so it is worth clarifying up front.

To review, the scope identified in each example is as follows:

- CLABSI example: "…among all patients admitted to our department between January and June of this year who required a central line."
- Insurance company example: "…to quantify the yearly benefits from the member perspective."

In the CLABSI example, the time frame and patient population are clearly stated; in the insurance company example, one quickly infers from context that the "patients" are the members themselves.

8.3.2.1 Framing the Scope as an Opportunity

This is perhaps an appropriate place to introduce a common scenario for framing the scope in a way that clearly demonstrates the potential value that could be realized. To illustrate, let us consider the example mentioned previously where a device company believed they could improve medication adherence among community-dwelling adults with uncontrolled hypertension.

If the device company aims to convince a health plan or investor that their product has merit, they can frame the scope by identifying and specifying a specific gap in care and then suggest the amount of that gap their device would address. To do this, they would need to leverage published estimates from research studies and impose a specific scope into their analysis. As illustrated in Table 8.4, this may involve a series of estimates, such as the prevalence of hypertension within community-dwelling adults, the percentage of those whose hypertension is still uncontrolled despite receiving the appropriate therapy (i.e., one or more antihypertensive medication), the percentage of those who are "likely" to have uncontrolled hypertension because of nonadherence, as opposed to being treatment-resistant, and the assumed additional cost due to the increased risk of adverse events.

In this way, the device company can frame the scope of its value assessment as addressing a specific need within a specialized population, as opposed to presenting the scope as only addressing a portion of the larger issue of uncontrolled hypertension. Said another way, the device company can identify this specific subgroup of all participants as an opportunity to realize value for the payer: Improve this group's medication adherence and lower their healthcare utilization and costs that stem from poor hypertension control.

Framing the scope as an opportunity to realize value sets the stage for the specific solution the company proposes: Their adherence-improving device. This technique can help direct the intended audience to focus on the specific patient population that is relevant for a particular product or device. This can be particularly effective for

Table 8.4 An Example of framing the scope as an opportunity

Component of the care gap	Estimated scope per 1000 members	Source[a]
Percent of patients with hypertension	60% = 600 members	Smith et al. (2018)
Percent whose hypertension is uncontrolled	50% of those with hypertension = 300 members	Nelson et al. (2019)
Percent whose uncontrolled hypertension may be due to nonadherence	20–60% = 60–180 members	Abrim et al. (2017)
Increased risk of stroke	10 more strokes per year	Silverstein et al. (2010)
Incremental cost per additional stroke	$10,000–$50,000 per year	Anderson et al. (2015)
And so on		

[a]These studies are not real

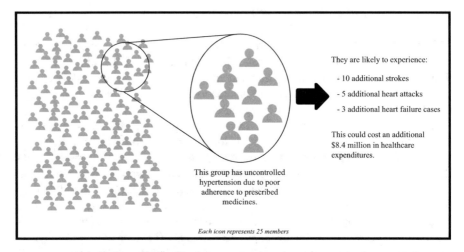

They are likely to experience:

- 10 additional strokes

- 5 additional heart attacks

- 3 additional heart failure cases

This could cost an additional
$8.4 million in healthcare
expenditures.

This group has uncontrolled
hypertension due to poor
adherence to prescribed
medicines.

Each icon represents 25 members

Fig. 8.2 An example of framing the scope as an opportunity. Note: The numbers in this figure are hypothetical and not based on clinical evidence

value assessments aimed at targeting high-risk individuals. Often, this can be where solutions offer the biggest improvement and most impressive benefit.

Alternatively, consider the situation where a device or med-tech company is seeking to be acquired or bought out by a larger entity. This may merit a slight adjustment to the scope because while the acquiring company will be interested in the potential for the solution to either save payers money or produce better patient outcomes, they may also be interested in market capture. That is, perhaps the acquiring company has a device that is specific to a particular clinical space, one where patients are known to frequently fall out of the therapeutic pathway (i.e., "lost to follow-up") or fail to progress to subsequent lines of therapy when appropriate. The smaller device company may have a solution that will, among other things, improve patient retention and/or progression along the clinical pathway, thereby increasing the potential market capture as it relates to the acquiring entity's own device or solution.

8.3.3   Question 3: What Is the Value Assessment's Goal or Objective? What Decision Will It Inform?

Often, a decision is on the horizon or a specific goal is being sought where a better understanding of the underlying value of one or more alternatives would be beneficial. This may be the motivation for performing a value assessment.

Understanding and specifying why it is beneficial to assess the value and how decision makers will use the results can and should inform how value is defined.

The stated goal of an assessment can inform what constitutes a relevant scope and/ or perspective. Similarly, getting clear about the scope and perspective will allow for further refinement of the stated goals. In the CLABSI example, the goal is to demonstrate a positive financial return for the investment made to reduce CLABSIs. Clearly, this goal informs the appropriate time frame and patient population. But, as we stated previously, there might be multiple appropriate patient populations (i.e., only those with central lines versus all patients in the department); once we settle on a specific patient population, our goal more fully takes shape.

In the CLABSI example, the financial return is limited to that which is directly associated with CLABSI reduction, ignoring any spillover that may have occurred that resulted in lower rates of other infections in other patients. So the goal of a positive financial return is more clearly defined as the financial return from CLABSI-related activities only.

We must be aware of two common pitfalls when specifying the goals of an assessment or the decision we wish to inform. The first pitfall is considering too many goals. One may assume that a single value assessment can inform a variety of value-based objectives, questions, or decisions, but that may not be the case. It is likely that different goals will require different scopes, metrics, or methods, and trying to develop an analysis that addresses all the goals will probably end up not informing any of them very well. In the insurance company example, it is notable that the described assessment does not also try to incorporate the value to the insurance company of the added coverage. It is implied that a previous assessment was done illustrating the financial return from the insurance company's perspective. It would be difficult to fully and clearly address the value to both the payer's perspective and the patient's, so a conscious decision was made to examine them separately.

The other common mistake is that the goal lacks specificity or detail. General goals like "increase revenue" or "determine how best to invest this year's budget" may be real but they do not provide much guidance for what activities or initiatives might address them. Instead, the goals and related decisions for how to reach those goals should be specific and provide as much detail as possible.

Some examples of decisions a value assessment may inform include:

- Will investment A or investment B result in a better return in the first 12 months?
- How many falls will this intervention need to prevent each month to break even within 6 months?
- Which components of the last investment produced the largest portion of the benefits; which cost the most?

Some examples of effective goal statements include:

- Goal: to convince this health plan to cover and pay for our device for all diabetic patients referred by their primary care physician
- Goal: to raise at least $3 million in seed money from five different investors
- Goal: to improve our facility's brand and reputation in a tangible way
- Goal: to convince the board of the worth of a previous investment in quality improvement and to fund future initiatives

By framing the question or goals where it is clear what a "success" would be makes it easier to ensure that the scope and perspective are appropriate; this will also make it obvious whether metrics exist that would measure that success.

In our CLABSI example, the goal of the initiative was expressed as follows:

- "Our goal for this analysis is to determine…whether the internal costs incurred to implement a comprehensive 'prevention bundle' produced a positive financial return."

And, while not explicitly stated within the executive summary, those performing the value assessment also aimed to convince board members of the value of the initiative in the hopes that they would be more likely to approve future quality improvement initiatives.

In the insurance company example, the goal was also explicitly stated:

- "Our goal is to attract and retain more plan members by clearly illustrating value to current and potential members."

The intent of the assessment is clear upon reading that statement, and we immediately know what to measure to evaluate its success.

8.3.4   Question 4: What Assumptions Will Be Made in the Value Assessment?

Explicitly stating the assumptions used in the value assessment is not only helpful for the intended audience, but such explicit statements can serve as a check to those developing and conducting value assessments about whether their underlying assumptions are reasonable. At times, we may be reluctant to state assumptions because they may be obviously false. In the CLABSI example, a stated assumption was that "100% of the reduction in CLABSI rates was directly due to the intervention." Given all we have explored to this point regarding the complexity of care delivery and the human element inherent in providing care, this statement seems unreasonable, at the very least. However, explicitly stating it is much preferred to implicitly relying on it when it comes time to calculate the associated benefits realized from the intervention. Stating the assumption demonstrates that you are aware of it and understand its implications. In the CLABSI example, those conducting the analysis could even explore alternative levels of attribution to see how much it affects the realized value. Failing to explicitly state the assumption invites critiques and can undermine the integrity of the assessment and its interpretation.

Examples of value assessments exist where key assumptions were left implicit, resulting in targeted and critical rebukes from outside evaluators. Several federal quality monitoring programs, for example, use some version of 30-day readmission rates and 30-day mortality rates as part of the quality measure suite that ranks and assesses participating hospitals and determines reimbursement bonuses or penalties. Although not specifically stated anywhere (to my knowledge), the assumptions required for reimbursement programs like this include:

- The validity and reliability of the measures used to compare the quality of facilities or physicians are adequate to inform reimbursement.
- Any and all readmissions are avoidable if a high enough level of quality is achieved.
- Improvements or changes in performance during the program's observation period will be considered independent of any prior existing trends that may have existed.
- 100% of observed change or improvement will be attributed to direct efforts made by hospitals and physicians participating in the program.

Subsequent to the federal programs' initiations, studies emerged challenging the validity and reliability of the readmission and mortality measures. Critics claimed that quality at the point of care was only partially responsible for what happened after discharge, and that many of the other factors were simply out of the hands of hospitals and their physicians. Additionally, differences in case mix, location, resources, patient population, and other characteristics made it impossible to fairly compare different facilities or physicians, even with risk adjustment methods applied. Shots were taken at the other (implicit) assumptions as well: Not all hospitalizations within 30 days were avoidable…some were even planned; rates of mortality were declining prior to the program and therefore some reduction observed during the program may have been due to the pre-existing trend or other activities that were separate from the program.

It is crucial to recognize and acknowledge the assumptions so that we can fully understand the definition of value used for a particular assessment and accurately make comparisons to other initiatives or activities. In the examples presented at the start of this chapter, multiple assumptions are made. As mentioned previously, the assessors in the CLABSI example state that they are assuming that 100% of the observed reduction in CLABSIs is due to the intervention. Alternatively, if they knew of other potential influencing factors, such as simultaneous interventions to improve patient safety or an upcoming audit by a regulatory body that could heighten staff's attention to the matter, they could have made an assumption regarding what portion of the reduction is due to the targeted intervention. Along the same lines, if they had intended to include value from spillover effects of the intervention on reductions in other safety measures, they would need to make an assumption regarding the attribution of those reductions to the CLABSI reduction intervention.

The assessors in the CLABSI example also had to make assumptions regarding how much revenue would be realized from an improvement in CLABSI quality measure performance. While not explicitly stated in the executive summary, the assumptions used to arrive at a monetary quantity would need to be specified. Finally, assessors made assumptions if and when they made extrapolations regarding the sustainability and therefore continued reductions in CLABSIs going forward. Even if these seem obvious, it helps to enumerate them so that it is clear what the value calculations are based on.

For the private insurance company increasing coverage on mental and behavioral health services, they have made similar assumptions; namely, that expected improvement in relevant patient outcomes (increased quality of life, reduced likelihood of more serious care utilization) is "directly and 100% attributed to the additional coverage" for specific services. For any audience, those performing the assessment will need to determine whether it is enough to simply state the assumptions or if evidence is required to support the assumptions being made. In this case, the insurance company will have to decide whether they believe current or potential plan members will find their assumptions reasonable without evidence or whether they would be more likely to believe value claims if the assumptions are evidence based.

8.3.5   *Who Is the Intended Audience for the Value Assessment?*

As with the previous step regarding goals and/or decisions, the intended audience may be obvious from the very start. However, as with the other components, carefully considering this question can produce more specificity; in turn, this may refine the other components of the value definition of, and lay a solid foundation for, the rest of the assessment.

As with setting the goal(s) for the assessment, it is tempting to try to develop an assessment that speaks to everyone. When posed the question about the intended audience, some of my clients have responded, "Well, primarily payers and providers, but we would also like it to be patient-facing and be informative and educational for them, too." While this is an understandable aim, the patient perspective on value will likely differ significantly from that of payers or providers and therefore something that is directed at one audience is rarely effective for another.

Here again I will point out that the order in which these components of the value definition are presented in this book are not necessarily the order in which you will address them. Most likely, you will consider all of them in tandem; and from a practical standpoint, you may find it helpful to list all the components on a blank table so that you can fill in the details as they become apparent.

In our examples, we discussed the intended audience from the start. For the CLABSI example, the audience is the hospital board, while for the example of the private insurer the audience is current and potential plan members.

With this accumulated information, the definition of what value represents in each example is clear to anyone. Additionally, these clear definitions will inform what costs and benefits are relevant, what metrics may be useful, and what the results mean for the goal or potential decision needing to be made.

8.4   Step 2 of the Value Assessment Framework: Determine Costs, Benefits, and Metrics

Often, those performing value assessments will skip the majority of what was described in Step 1 and dive right into the endeavor of quantifying costs and benefits; they do this so that they can calculate metrics they hope will inform their decision or guide their activity. But, without clearly defining value in terms of the scope, perspective, goals, assumptions, and audience, value assessments that jump straight to identifying costs and benefits typically need to pause and retroactively define the aspects described in the previous section.

I believe you will find that if you want to explore costs, benefits, and metrics until after you have set the stage as described in the previous section, you will see that this process is much easier and more effective for providing the most appropriate and useful information for your stated goals.

8.4.1   Define Costs and Benefits

8.4.1.1   Costs

Defining costs (within the framework of the scope and perspective already defined) involves specifying the following:

- The source of the costs
- The measurement and quantification of the costs
- The level of attribution of costs to the change/process/product/and so on

Often, identifying and quantifying costs is straightforward. For example, when assessing the value of a CMS- or payer-funded quality improvement initiative, the costs from those perspectives may simply be the funding amount, measured in monetary currency (e.g., dollars), and fully attributable to the targeted intervention.

Other times, however, identifying and quantifying costs may not be so clear. For example, if assessing the value of telehealth from a patient perspective, relevant costs will be those patients incur and for the particular scope defined regarding a specific telehealth intervention, process, or solution. Depending on the situation, cost sources may include those related to having access to telehealth (e.g., internet access, a usable device, etc.) and/or the time and effort needed to learn the functionality of the solution and actually participating in a telehealth visit. You would likely measure or quantify these costs using monetary quantities and units of time spent. However, other cost sources may be relevant for the patient. Examples include risks associated with not having a face-to-face visit with their provider (e.g., no physical exam is possible, perhaps patients feel less of a human connection to their provider, etc.) and costs associated with coupled health encounters (e.g., perhaps they need to visit the clinic to have blood drawn even though most of their visit took place virtually).

Not all identified costs may be feasible to include in the assessment but having a structure for how to define them can help you think through the possibilities and consider when they are relevant or to what extent you can attribute them to the chosen change, process, product, or intervention. That is, if determining whether the cost of an internet connection is relevant when assessing the value of a telehealth intervention, we not only need to determine whether we can measure and quantify it but also whether its cost is attributable to the intervention. If an individual already has an adequate internet connection and uses it for more than just the telehealth intervention, perhaps we decide that the cost of that person's internet connection is not attributable to the intervention and exclude it from the assessment.

In our examples, we assume the cost of the CLABSI intervention from the provider perspective to be anything that is "directly related to the planning, preparation, and implementation of the prevention bundle." More than likely the bulk of this cost would be comprised of materials, training, and staff time, all of which could likely be quantified and monetized. This is important since the organization is interested in assessing the financial return associated with the implementation of the prevention bundle. There may also be some costs of collecting, analyzing, and disseminating data as part of the initiative.

Regarding attribution, while not specifically stated in our two examples' executive summaries, we can reasonably assume that 100% of these costs would be attributable to the initiative unless some of the materials or activities could be thought to be applied to something else. For example, if software was purchased to help track and chart progress of the initiative, but the hospital plans to use that software for other initiatives, perhaps in the assessment it would be reasonable to only attribute some of the cost to the CLABSI intervention. For the insurance company offering increased coverage of mental and behavioral health services, the relevant monetary and nonmonetary costs are those the patient incurs since the value assessment is done from the patient perspective.

As noted in the example's description, it is difficult for the insurance company to know or estimate what those costs may be. For current members, we assume the incremental costs compared to what they would pay to be zero since premiums did not rise as a direct result of the added coverage. This does not mean that patient costs do not exist. Some members may incur an indirect cost by choosing to remain members as opposed to, say, switching to their spouse's insurance. The costs to those individuals of staying with their current plans instead of switching would be unknown to the insurance company that is hoping they will remain members. For potential members, too, while there may exist costs associated with becoming members, the insurance company likely will not know what those costs for members are relative to their other options (i.e., other health insurance or forgoing insurance).

8.4.1.2   Benefits

As with costs, defining benefits requires an identification of their source, their measurement or quantification, and their attribution. Often, defining benefits is more complicated than defining costs. However, for the most part, the sources of potential benefits from improvements in care delivery, processes, or the introduction of a new product, device, or innovation fall into one of five categories:

- Utilization
- Efficiency
- Patient experience or health

- Administrative
- Societal

Overlap exists between some of the categories because many are closely related. For example, reducing infections may produce a benefit related to lower utilization, but it would also lead to better patient outcomes, improved patient experiences, and a better facility reputation, all of which are in other categories. Let us explore each of these categories more fully.

Utilization

Benefits related to utilization reflect a reduced "need" for care resulting from higher quality care or improved patient health. This category encompasses much of what healthcare professionals strive for when improving care or introducing a new treatment or device. In addition to decreases in utilization, reducing the *risk* of utilization also belongs in this category. Most benefits related to utilization are measurable and quantifiable; also, they are often attributable to a specific intervention or change. Common types of benefits related to utilization include:

- Lower incidence or prevalence of disease
- Fewer (actual or risk of) adverse events or need for health encounters
- Lower intensity of care or length of care (e.g., length of stay, use of ICU, fewer medications, faster recovery, etc.)

Most often, lower utilization is a benefit for payers, but it may also provide benefit from the perspectives of patients, caregivers, providers, and society.[1]

Efficiency and Reduced Waste

Benefits in this category overlap some with those in the utilization category. For example, if a new and improved care protocol reduces the need for redundant lab tests, we could consider that as lower utilization, but we could also consider it to simply be more efficient care; there is less waste (redundancy) because fewer unnecessary tests are performed. Benefits related to efficiency also tend to include value to a facility, such as a hospital, for care that is reimbursed by a bundled payment. If care can be provided more efficiently, the hospital spends less money caring for the patient while still receiving the full reimbursement amount. Efficiency-related benefits are usually measurable and quantifiable, but sometimes attribution to a specific cause can be challenging. Examples include:

- Lower resource use (e.g., fewer lab tests, less time in OR)
- Fewer treatment errors

---

[1] In general, the benefits listed have potential benefits to third-party healthcare organizations (TPHOs) that seek to sell their solution to payers, providers, and/or patients because of the benefits those entities realize through the use of the TPHO's solution.

- "Faster" care (e.g., shorter wait times, faster time-to-treatment)
- Better/more accurate diagnosis
- More continuous care, less discontinuation of care/therapy, less duplication in care or services
- Better use of staff time, appropriate level of full-time equivalents (FTEs), less turnover, and so on

Typically, better efficiency provides benefits to payers and/or providers, but it may also provide benefits to patients, caregivers, and society.

Patient Experience and/or Health

This broad category includes everything from the satisfaction a patient has with their care experience and their relationship with the health system to the quality of life and well-being that results from care. These days, we can use tools to measure many patient experience and/or health benefits, but they are not always measured. Whether they are quantifiable is variable and often depends on the perspective used. Examples of this type of benefit include:

- Improved health and/or quality of life (increased survival, lower disease severity, quality-adjusted life years, slower disease progression, reduced symptom burden, fewer side effects, etc.)
- Higher satisfaction (with care quality, with provider, with care experience, etc.)
- Improved trust (e.g., patient–clinician relationship, level of communication/honesty, etc.)
- More patient engagement/self-efficacy
- Reduced disease burden (e.g., pill burden, comorbidity burden, life interference, etc.)
- Improved emotional/psychological/physical/social well-being (everything from level of depression/anxiety to things like confidence, peace of mind, gratitude, functioning, socialization, isolation/loneliness, etc.)
- Reduced caregiver burden

These examples usually reflect benefits to patients as well as their families and caregivers. Often, some amount of indirect benefit exists for providers that may manifest as improved job satisfaction or increased efficiency. Payers may also experience value indirectly since addressing patient experience and/or health benefits may boost member retention or reflect better population health, which in turn can result in lower utilization. Clearly, there is societal benefit as well.

Administrative

The administrative category includes anything and everything that a facility or care delivery system may receive benefits from. Increases in revenue or reductions in costs associated with the "business" of delivering care are sometimes the primary goal of an intervention or change, but sometimes they are a bonus that comes from providing better or more efficient care. Examples of administrative benefits include:

- Increased revenue from risk pools or from performance-based reimbursement mechanisms
- Patient/member retention
- New patient/member initiation
- Reduced (actual or risk of) litigation
- Improved brand or reputation
- Increased regulatory compliance
- Reduced facility/equipment costs

Most often, healthcare providers are the ones who realize administrative benefits.

Societal

Societal benefits are not always considered and by their nature can be difficult to measure. Further, it can be difficult to differentiate societal benefits from those linked to the patient or their caregiver. For example, a healthier patient probably has less work absenteeism and higher productivity, but one could argue whether those are societal or personal benefits. Examples of societal benefits include:

- Increased work productivity
- Reduced work absenteeism
- Increased societal output
- Improved equity (in all aspects)
- Reduced criminal justice system burden
- Reduced need for social safety nets (components of this might be viewed as improved efficiency of social spending and resource allocations)

As the name implies, societal benefits typically result in benefit for society as a whole.

This is not an exhaustive list but represents the majority of potential benefits in most situations. And, even if this list represented the universe of possible benefit sources, issues of their measurement, quantification, and attribution would still exist. In general, it is difficult to include a benefit in an assessment if it isn't: measurable, quantifiable, and attributable (at least in part) to the solution being examined (Table 8.5).

Once we identify the sources of benefits, we need to determine to what extent we can attribute the benefit to the change, process, product, or intervention. If it is unreasonable to assume 100% attribution, we can make "adjustments" or alternate assumptions regarding the percent attribution. In the CLABSI example, instead of attributing 100% of changes in infection rates to a particular intervention, we could try to account for:

- The previously existing trend in infection rates prior to the intervention

Table 8.5 The most common benefit sources

Category	Examples of benefits
Utilization	Lower incidence or prevalence of disease
	Fewer (actual or risk of) adverse events or need for health encounters
	Lower intensity of care or length of care (e.g., length of stay, use of ICU, fewer medications, faster recovery)
Efficiency and reduced waste	Lower resource use (e.g., fewer lab tests, less time in OR)
	Fewer treatment errors
	"Faster" care (e.g., shorter wait times, faster time-to-treatment)
	Better/more accurate diagnosis
	More continuous care, less discontinuation of care/therapy, less duplication in care or services
	Better use of staff time, appropriate level of FTEs, less turnover
Patient experience and/or health	Improved health and/or quality of life (increased survival, lower disease severity, quality-adjusted life years, slower disease progression, reduced symptom burden, fewer side effects, etc.)
	Higher satisfaction (with care quality, with provider, with care experience, etc.)
	Improved trust (e.g., patient–clinician relationship, level of communication/honesty, etc.)
	More patient engagement/self-efficacy
	Reduced disease burden (e.g., pill burden, comorbidity burden, life interference, etc.)
	Improved emotional/psychological/physical/social well-being (everything from level of depression/anxiety to things like confidence, peace of mind, gratitude, functioning, socialization, isolation/loneliness, etc.)
	Reduced caregiver burden
Administrative	Increased revenue from risk pools or from performance-based reimbursement mechanisms
	Patient/member retention
	New patient/member initiation
	Reduced (actual or risk of) litigation
	Improved brand or reputation
	Increased regulatory compliance
	Reduced facility/equipment costs
Societal	Increased work productivity
	Reduced work absenteeism
	Increased societal output
	Improved equity (in all aspects)
	Reduced criminal justice system burden
	Reduced need for social safety nets

- Other common factors that may influence changes in rates (additional initiatives, policies, changes in guidelines, external factors, etc.)
- Random and natural variation that occurs anytime something is measured

When we seek financial value, I have suggested focusing on sources of value that are measurable, monetizable, and attributable to the intervention, product, process, change, or initiative we seek to evaluate. For other types of value, obviously it will be unnecessary to identify monetizable sources of value, but they should at least be quantifiable in some way, even if through subjective opinion or judgments (e.g., a scale such as "poor," "fair," "good," "excellent," or even simply "better" versus "worse"). The other two criteria—measurable and attributable—still hold for nonfinancial value.

As stated previously, for the CLABSI reduction initiative, the benefits are:

- "the estimated increase in reimbursement revenue from quality monitoring programs that use CLABSI as one of the criteria to determine reimbursement".

Additional value may also come from the potential for improved brand and reputation in the community. As described in the example's executive summary, the former is quantifiable while the latter is not. In the insurance company example, benefits to patients reflect the reduced cost of the covered mental and behavioral health services, lower likelihood of the need for more intensive treatment (which has monetary and nonmonetary benefits), and any "feel-good" benefits members would experience because of being covered by a plan that shows that the insurance company understands the importance of mental and behavioral health.

8.4.2 Explore Various Metrics

At this point, after establishing our value definition, we have identified the appropriate sources and quantities of costs and benefits. At this point, it is appropriate to determine how we will associate costs and benefits through the choice of metrics. A variety of metrics exist related to the value of healthcare services, improvements, and the like. Many are used in other industries and will be known to you, but you should be aware of the nuances in using them in health care. The appropriate metric(s) for a given assessment will depend on the aspects of the assessment addressed to this point, including the perspective, scope, goal/objective, and audience. Rarely does a single metric adequately measure and/or convey the entirety of the value or its interpretation. Using multiple metrics allows us to consider value in different lights and often encourages different thinking or comparisons that are not possible when using only a single metric. The typical metrics used in value assessments of health care are presented in the following section in no particular order.

8.4.2.1 ROI and BCR

Return on investment (ROI) and the benefit to cost ratio (BCR) are closely linked and reflect a similar sentiment: the magnitude of the accrued benefits relative to the associated costs. ROI considers benefits net costs as a percentage of the costs, while the BCR is simply the ratio of the benefits to the costs (as the name implies). Specifically:

$$ROI = (Benefits - Costs) / Costs \times 100\%$$

(8.1)

And

$$BCR = Benefits / Costs$$

(8.2)

So, using an example presented elsewhere: [1] If $25,000 in costs is incurred to secure $35,000 in benefits, then

$$ROI = (\$35,000 - \$25,000) / \$25,000 \times 100\% = 40\%$$

And

$$BCR = \$35,000 / \$25,000 = 1.4$$

The interpretation of ROI may seem more intuitive at first, in part because it is the same calculation performed in banking and finance, which most people are familiar with. However, the BCR allows for an interpretation of the form "For every $1 spent there was a benefit of $1.40," which can also be appealing when relaying results to particular audiences. We can encourage this interpretation by writing the BCR using different notation, such as:

- 1.4/1
- 1.4 to 1
- 1.4:1
- $1.40:$1.00

Note that one potentially confusing difference is that while the break-even point (where benefits equal costs) is reflected by an ROI of 0% but a BCR of 1. Even in the literature, this point has been misconstrued at times in part by using the terms BCR and ROI interchangeably or defining their calculation incorrectly and then claiming that a result <1 reflects a negative return.[2] The message here is to take care when you write or present the results, and *always* clearly define the metrics and show your work so that there is no confusion.

Another potential source of confusion when dealing with monetary units is the distinction between "benefits" and "net benefits." When measuring the effectiveness of any improvement or solution, attributable benefits will be incremental beyond what existed prior to implementation, but that does not imply that those benefits are "net" of anything. When performing these calculations, "net benefits" *always* means "benefits net of costs" (i.e., benefits minus costs) which is the difference between attributable benefits and attributable costs. Again, we can easily avoid any confusion

---

[2] I provide a much more comprehensive look at ROI and BCR in the 2020 book, *Return on Investment for Healthcare Quality Improvement* (Springer), and therefore I do not go into extensive detail here.

by using clear definitions and providing transparent details of calculations and any formulas used.

There are no hard and fast rules for when to use ROI versus BCR, but there are some general guidelines to consider.

1. When the return is very large, say over 1000%, it can be difficult to conceptualize a return that large or make reasonable comparisons in one's head; however, representing the same return as the BCR can seem more concrete. For example, consider where the ROI is calculated as 9900%; that can be hard to imagine, but it is much easier to think about when expressed as a BCR of $100 in benefit for each $1 spent, which is equivalent to an ROI of 9900%.
2. I have heard it said that when people hear ROI they think in terms of a lump sum one-time investment, while the interpretation of BCR implies that each additional dollar you wish to put toward an initiative or healthcare solution will continue to produce the stated return; I don't know that I agree, but you should at least be aware of the different interpretations that exist.
3. ROI may be more familiar to administrators or those involved in making financial decisions and therefore may be preferred for those audiences.

Also note that ROI and BCR are highly dependent on the defined time frame of the assessment since extending the time frame would potentially allow for more time to accrue benefits and/or incur costs. The appropriate time frame is not always obvious; sometimes, there are "ramp-up" or preparatory periods prior to the implementation of a change in process or the introduction of a new system or product, and it may be unclear how much of that prior period should be included (as stated previously: determining what is attributable can be difficult). Therefore, always report ROI and BCR in relation to the time period they reflect: "the ROI over the first year of the program was 34%…"

Net Value

You will likely encounter the term "net value," which most often reflects the exact same thing as net benefits defined previously. That is, it is simply the difference between benefits and costs (which is the numerator of the ROI calculation).

Payback Period

As stated previously, ROI and BCR are closely tied to the time frame so that different time frames often produce different values (in fact, one component you can choose to vary in a sensitivity analysis is the time frame). The payback period is a metric that is not dependent on a select time period. It is defined as follows:

$$\text{Payback Period} = \text{Costs} / \left(\text{Benefits per Unit of Time} \right)$$

(8.3)

A payback period is a unit of time, such as months, quarters, or years. So, extending our previous example where the costs were \$25,000, if we accrued benefits at a rate of \$2500 per month, the payback period (the point at which accrued benefits equal total costs) would be 10 months. If, however, we continued to incur additional costs over that time, we would need to include them and so our payback period would be a bit longer.

The payback period can be a useful metric in prospective analyses where planning is essential; it can also be useful in retrospective assessments when the current ROI is negative. As in, "after six months the ROI is negative, but with an expected payback period of ten months, we anticipate that a positive return will begin in four months."

Savings per Unit

A number of metrics are simply variations of ROI, BCR, or their components. For example, savings per unit (e.g., per patient, per facility, etc.) simply divides the net benefits by the number of units affected. This can help put spending and saving in perspective, especially for large programs: The total savings may be in the tens of millions of dollars, but if spread over two million patients across the country, then stating that the savings were \$5 per patient frames the "success" of the program in a different light.

8.4.2.2   Cost per Unit Benefit

The BCR reflects the amount of benefits per unit of cost. If you flip those quantities, you get the costs needed to achieve one unit of benefit (Fig. 8.3). The definition of cost per unit benefit is shown in Eq. (8.4).

$$\text{Cost per Unit Benefit} = (\text{Total Cost}) / (\text{Total Benefits})$$

$$(8.4)$$

Costs may be monetary or in terms of time, resources, personnel, or some other unit, and benefits will typically be nonmonetary, such as the number of events avoided, the number of additional patients treated, life years added, or some other quantifiable benefit.

To illustrate, consider an ED that wants to employ new systems and processes to reduce patient wait times with the ultimate goal of lowering the number of patients who leave without being seen (LWBS). Estimating the monetary cost of each patient who LWBS can be problematic, as it often depends on acuity, time of day, age,

$$\text{BCR} = \frac{\text{Benefits}}{\text{Costs}} \times \frac{\text{Costs}}{\text{Benefits}} = \frac{\text{Cost per}}{\text{Unit Benefit}}$$

Fig. 8.3 The relationship between BCR and cost per unit benefit

Table 8.6 Example calculation of cost per unit benefit

	Strategy #1	Strategy #2
Additional FTEs needed	1.5	0
Additional materials	None	Electronic decision tool
Costs	$60,000	$30,000
LWBS events avoided	250	150
Cost per unit benefit	$240 per LWBS avoided	$200 per LWBS avoided

Assume LWBS events and costs are on an annual basis

insurance status, and so on. Therefore, the ED may want a metric that incorporates LWBS as simply the number of such events without assigning a dollar value to it. The benefit of an effective strategy to reduce wait times would be a reduction in the number of LWBS events. To evaluate the value of possible strategies, we could consider the cost of each compared to the size of the reduction in LWBS events each would produce. Imagine that the ED is considering two alternative strategies:

- Possible Strategy #1: A new triage process that would employ an additional 1.0 to 2.0 FTEs
- Possible Strategy #2: A new electronic clinical decision tool that would not require any additional FTEs but would require resources to train staff and of course to purchase and integrate the tool into its current system

If the ED were to test (or estimate) the potential impact of each possible strategy, they could obtain the number of LWBS events each strategy avoids along with the cost to implement each (even though those costs have very different sources). For each option, dividing the total cost of implementation by the number of LWBS events avoided would produce a cost per LWBS avoided. In that way, without assigning a cost to each LWBS event, they could compare which option would produce the lowest cost per event avoided. Table 8.6 illustrates how these calculations could be performed.

In this example, it is probably straightforward to translate FTEs into dollars, but sometimes translating either costs or benefits into monetary terms is problematic. In such cases, it may be reasonable to leave costs in nonmonetary terms: If in our example the ED was considering two possible strategies that both incorporated additional FTEs, costs could be left in terms of FTEs and the cost per unit benefit could be directly compared between the two scenarios even though neither costs nor benefits are in terms of dollars.

It is also the case that when left in nonmonetary terms, the results may be immediately relevant for multiple perspectives. Consider an intervention, device, or process that attempts to reduce medication errors among community-dwelling adults. Assessing the value of such a solution (regardless of the perspective) would likely involve the potential avoidance of adverse events that are associated with poor adherence. In some cases, medication errors can result in an ED visit, hospitalization stay, or even death. If the intervention, device, or process was successful in

Table 8.7 Example, Part 1: Reducing adverse events caused by medication errors

	Scenario A	Scenario B
Inputs		
Total cost	$25,000	$35,000
Hospitalizations avoided	5	6
ED visits avoided	8	12
Calculations		
Cost per hospitalization avoided	$5000[a]	$5833
Cost per ED visit avoided	$3125	$2917[a]
Sum	$8125[a]	$8750

a Indicates the better value

reducing medication errors, some useful metrics based on the cost per unit benefit may be:

- Monetary cost per death avoided = (total costs)/(total number of deaths avoided).[3]
- Number of devices per medication error avoided = (total number of devices employed)/(total number of errors avoided).

Not only is the monetary "value" of a death avoided somewhat difficult to assign, whatever that value is would differ significantly from a payer or provider perspective versus from a patient perspective. Leaving the metric in terms of the raw, non-monetary benefit allows us to determine the value for multiple perspectives without navigating the difficulties of estimating the economic value of a human life.

However, when monetary values are available for both the costs and the benefits, it is instructive to explore how a cost per unit benefit metric differs from those we have explored previously.

Consider an extension of the medication error device just explored, where the outcomes of interest are reductions in error-related ED visits and hospitalizations, and the perspective of interest is that of a payer. Table 8.7 describes the basic inputs of two alternative scenarios, which could be for different populations, different interventions, different devices, or some other decision or comparison.

Note that the number of hospitalizations and ED visits avoided in Scenario A are lower but so are the costs to realize those benefits. When we divide the total costs by the number of events avoided, the cost per unit benefit is better (lower) in Scenario A for both hospitalizations but is better (lower) in Scenario B for ED visits.

The assessment really gets interesting if we assume an average cost avoidance (i.e., a savings for each event avoided) of $8500 for each hospitalization and $3500 for each ED visit. With these values (and now monetary values for both costs and

---

[3] Depending on the situation, it may be reasonable to assume that both costs and deaths would be standardized to a specific population size, so that they were actually rates per 1000 patient months, or something similar.

Table 8.8 Example, Part 2: Reducing adverse events caused by medication errors

	Scenario A	Scenario B
Inputs		
Total cost	$25,000	$35,000
Hospitalizations avoided	5	6
ED visits avoided	8	12
Cost savings: Hospitalizations avoided	$8500	$8500
Cost savings: ED visits avoided	$3500	$3500
Calculations		
Cost per hospitalization avoided	$5000[a]	$5833
Cost per ED visit avoided	$3125	$2917[a]
Sum	$8125[a]	$8750
Net cost[b] per hospitalization avoided	−$3500[a]	−$2667
Net cost[b] per ED visit avoided	−$375	−$583[a]
Sum	−$3875[a]	−$3250
Total benefit (total events avoided × cost savings)	$70,500	$93,000[a]
Net benefit (total benefit − total cost)	$45,500	$58,000[a]
ROI (net benefit/total cost × 100%)	182%[a]	166%
BCR (total benefit/total cost)	2.82[a]	2.66

Using just the values in this table, we quickly see that Scenario B offers greater overall benefit and net benefit, but that Scenario A produces a better financial return
[a] Indicates the better value
[b] A negative net cost reflects a net benefit

benefits) we can look at the "net" cost per unit benefit and at what more traditional metrics like ROI would indicate. Table 8.8 contains the additional inputs and calculations. The only calculations that require additional detail are the net cost per adverse event avoided.

To calculate these metrics, we subtract the cost savings associated with the avoidance of each event from the cost per event avoided, so the Net Cost per Hospitalization Avoided in Scenario A is calculated as $5000 − $8500 = −$3500, and similarly for Scenario B. In this case, the greater the negative value the better because a negative net cost reflects a net benefit. In plain language, this metric reflects that on average the cost required to avoid each hospitalization is less than it would have cost to pay for that hospitalization, which suggests that the initiative was/is a good idea.

Additionally, in terms of comparisons, Scenario A produces a better net benefit than Scenario B for hospitalizations, while the opposite is true for ED Visits. Further, the incremental savings Scenario A provides per hospitalization avoided ($833) is greater than the incremental savings Scenario B provides per ED Visit avoided ($208); but ED visits are more common than hospitalizations. The determination of which scenario is "better" or has "more value" will be a function of the value definition developed for the analysis. Some would suggest that total benefits and net benefits are more important than the ROI; others would claim the opposite. This shows why the definition of value and the ultimate interpretation play such crucial roles. Just presenting the table of results to an audience may leave them unclear about which scenario is better.

This can be a dizzying amount of information to sort through, but it can also help us understand the causes driving the costs, benefits, and overall value. Consider at the bottom of Table 8.8 the aggregate measures of total and net benefit as well as ROI and BCR. Using just these values, we quickly see that Scenario B offers greater overall benefit and net benefit, but that Scenario A produces a better financial return. Those conflicting results may be difficult to sort through, but the additional metrics related to cost per unit benefit provide a better understanding of the value of each.

It should be noted that like the ROI-based metrics, this one may also be closely tied to a time frame, either by using rates per time at risk or by comparing the cost per unit benefit over comparable time frames.

By the way, a version of BCR could be calculated that does not include money. To illustrate, consider programs that attempt to improve chronic disease management by pairing patients with peer mentors. These programs have been effective in improving control of diseases like diabetes, and thus reduce diabetes hospitalizations and adverse events. Instead of considering the monetary components of either the costs or the benefits of these programs, we might calculate a metric like: Hospitalizations avoided per peer mentor recruited. In this way, we may be able to compare the value of these types of programs across different clinical topics.

Because our motivating example of reducing CLABSIs is interested in the financial return of the initiative to the payer, financial metrics such as ROI, BCR, or payback period are most appropriate to use. And, considering the audience of the hospital board and the goal of convincing the board to approve future initiatives, demonstrating the financial viability and positive return of such efforts seems like the best course of action. For the insurance company touting the value of their new coverage for mental and behavioral health services to current and potential members, a variety of metrics may be best. To start, they may want to calculate a simple out-of-pocket cost savings estimate that would be relevant to members who may need to use some of the covered services. But, they would likely want to also express value as a function of nonmonetary benefits, such as reduced work absenteeism and greater quality of life. Given that costs to members may be zero or unknown, it may not be possible to express these benefits per unit of cost to the member, but it may still be appropriate to use those metrics.

The Incremental Cost-Effectiveness Ratio

It may be illustrative for some readers to understand that the cost per unit benefit is essentially what the incremental cost-effectiveness ratio (ICER) represents in cost-effectiveness analysis. Specifically, the ICER is defined as:

$$ICER = (C_1 - C_0) / (E_1 - E_0)$$

$$(8.5)$$

where C and E reflect the costs and effectiveness, respectively, in the groups being compared. Often, C_0 and E_0 reflect the status quo, or usual care, and E is often quality-adjusted life years (QALYs), so that the calculation reflects the cost per QALY added. An advantage of the ICER and why it is so often used is that it represents a standard metric that can be compared across initiatives or topic areas. It makes sense to extend this concept and broaden it to reflect a value metric for other situations.

Additionally, we could use an ICER to compare the two scenarios just presented by calculating the difference in costs divided by the difference in effectiveness. When we do that, we see that the ICERs associated with Scenario B versus Scenario A are $10,000 per additional hospitalization avoided ($35,000 − $25,000)/(6 − 5), and $2500 per additional ED visit, by a similar calculation. The difficulty then is to determine when it is "worth it" to pay the additional cost to get the additional benefits. In this case, if we use the estimated utilization costs associated with each hospitalization and ED visit of $8500 and $3500, respectively, then it would be worth it for the ED visits (since the incremental cost of reducing a visit is less than the cost to pay for the visit) but not for the hospitalization (since the incremental cost exceeds the cost of a hospitalization).

8.4.3 Identify Relevant Benchmarks or Comparisons

When organizations attempt to quantify the financial benefits or the ROI of a particular activity, one of the most common questions is, "What's a good ROI?" The answer, invariably, is "It depends." However, just because universal benchmarks may not always exist does not mean that we should not look for them. On the contrary, very often the evaluation of the results of a value assessment involves a comparison of some kind. Therefore, in all value assessments—not just ROI—identifying relevant benchmarks and considering the appropriate comparison requires forethought and a strong understanding of how the assessment will be used.

Additionally, specifying the desired comparison can inform how we define value in a particular situation. If, for example, CMS wanted to laud the effectiveness or value of a program designed to reduce hospital readmissions, then multiple aspects, including the intended audience, the definition of value, and any comparisons would be relevant. Consider two (hypothetical) separate scenarios that could emerge from the exact same program information:

- **Scenario 1:** To justify spending on the program to *lawmakers* (the audience), CMS calculates the total monetary savings to the government (the definition of value) generated by the reduction in readmissions and notes that the savings are greater than any other single activity intended to reduce healthcare-related spending during the year (the comparison).
- **Scenario 2:** To gain public support for the program from the *general public* (the audience), CMS calculates the estimated number of readmissions avoided per

1000 citizens and the total number of hospital days avoided (the definition of value) and claims that the impact on keeping patients out of the hospital is similar to avoiding 10,000 car crashes (the comparison).

These may be extreme examples in terms of the hyperbole applied to the comparison, but even in more mundane situations, identifying a reasonable benchmark or comparison frames the results and may help persuade key stakeholders to make a particular decision. Reasonable comparisons may include previous attempts to improve care, results experienced at comparable sites or in similar situations elsewhere, or estimated value from alternative activities. If we define value in monetary terms, then a reasonable comparison may simply be the financial return we could expect from an alternative investment. For value defined in nonmonetary terms, it may be wise to seek comparisons that place the results in context; in the second scenario just presented, the comparison is to car crashes.

For the CLABSI reduction initiative example, benchmarks or comparisons may be the relevant monetary ones, such as the break-even point (i.e., an ROI of at least 0%) or the time until breakeven. However, since they want to persuade the board that the investment was good, perhaps a good comparison is the return realized from alternative financial investments. Maybe there were other initiatives they could have funded, other initiatives from the hospital's past, or some other alternative they can hold up next to the realized return to suggest its worth. For the insurance company adding coverage to certain mental and behavioral health services, there may not be an explicit comparison to make. However, the chosen metrics make an implicit comparison to what would be true without the coverage.

8.5   Step 3 of the Value Assessment Framework: Interpret and Communicate

No value assessment is complete without an interpretation of the results and an application of its findings toward a specific question or decision. Ultimately, the interpretation and communication of results determine whether anyone will see, understand, and care about what you have learned. Therefore, this step is critically important to assessing and comparing value.

Clearly communicating results should include details of the accumulated framework components. Part of the benefit of the framework is that it identifies the information that audiences need if they are to fully understand the motivation and methods of the value assessment. Therefore, if you use the framework to design and carry out your assessment, it is an easy exercise to pull the relevant information and place it in a report, presentation, or communication.

When interpreting the results for an audience, the details of the value definition, identified costs and benefits, and selected metrics provide the context for the interpretation. In the CLABSI example, the interpretation is that the intervention produced a positive financial return for the hospital. This interpretation is informative only when viewed in light of the targeted patient population, the time frame, the costs and benefits included, and so on. The interpretation can only inform future decisions when we fully understand the specifics of how it was determined. If the board from the CLABSI example is considering whether to fund another quality improvement initiative, the relevance of the results of the CLABSI initiative depends on how similar that initiative is to the one being considered. Correctly determining that relevance requires a full understanding of the components of both initiatives. Stated more directly, if the new initiative were going to be implemented in the same department, by the same staff, to the same patient population, over the same time period, using similar measures of costs and benefits, we might be more likely to use the CLABSI initiative as support for the likelihood of the success of the new initiative than if some or all of those components differed between the two initiatives.

Beyond the basic logic involved in interpreting results within the context of the components of the assessment, I believe in several basic tenets regarding value assessments that can guide the interpretation and dissemination of results. Each of these speaks to specific best practices for interpreting and communicating the results of your assessment effectively. While not every value assessment may contain all these practices, good ones will contain most of them.

8.5.1   Guiding Principles for Interpreting and Communicating Results

8.5.1.1   Explore All Types of Value

Principle #1: Value is more than the financial return. The motivation for improving systems of care or developing a new device or treatment is most often to positively impact patients. Regardless of the financial implications, much of the value of these activities stems from nonmonetary benefits. There is inherent value in good health, longevity, satisfaction, peace of mind, dignity, comfort, and so on. Certainly, the financial return indicates whether an activity or change is feasible, but rarely should one consider the financial return separately from value in the larger sense. Instead, we should interpret the financial component in light of the larger context of the situation and goals of those involved. A poor or negative ROI does not necessarily mean we should scrap the proposed solution or process; rather, it signals an incongruence between intrinsic value and financial realities. It should motivate questions like, "How do we reduce costs so that we can implement this process to help patients?" and "How can we more efficiently offer this tool that will allow providers to more acutely connect, understand, and care for their patients?" The financial return serves us best when viewed as a component of value and to direct our attention and next steps.

For the CLABSI reduction initiative, while the main source of value presented for the board will be financial, the most persuasive justification for the value of the initiative will include the improvements in brand and reputation as well as the improved patient care at the heart of the initiative. Aspects of the initiative may inform future initiatives so that some of the value comes from gained knowledge and experience related to implementing a care program that we can use to improve the process the next time. While not expressly defined in the framework or quantified through a metric, it may be valuable nonetheless and worth mentioning to the board. For the insurance company, current and potential members would likely appreciate both monetary and nonmonetary benefits from the increased coverage; and simply enumerating them would probably serve to inform and teach members more than they previously knew.

8.5.1.2   Inform, Guide, and Teach

Principle #2: A value assessment should do more than just restate what is already known. In a conversation with a client about how to frame the results of their assessment, I said, "If a value assessment is necessary to do, then the value is not obvious." The implication being that one should not waste anyone's time telling them what they already know. When communicating the results of a value assessment, simply reciting the quantities calculated and the calculated metrics does not guide, inform, or teach the audience anything they couldn't have ascertained from simply looking at a table in your results section.

Instead, describe the targeted analysis that addresses specific questions or issues, and walk the audience through the various steps to that end: assumptions and estimates used, calculations made, and the understanding revealed by the process. Welcome feedback and suggestions, even debate. Regardless of the specific goals, the objective of a value assessment is often to inform concrete decisions and help shape targeted actions. Therefore, those reading or hearing the results should learn something new, think of something in a different or more comprehensive way, or consider a provocative new perspective.

In the CLABSI example at the beginning of this chapter, perhaps an opportunity exists to teach the board how to consider and evaluate future proposals for quality improvement initiatives by showing them how the costs and benefits accrue and are accounted for or maybe simply by sharing the insights gained regarding how best to implement this type of initiative. For the insurance company example, the members and potential members may learn about the importance of the mental and behavioral health services and better understand the benefit we would get from them.

8.5.1.3   Merge Technical and Practical Considerations

Principle #3: Credible and compelling value assessments are a mixture of technical results and practical realities. I strongly believe that an effective assessment is both credible and compelling. Assessments that are too technical lack the ability to motivate or move the intended audience because the results can seem too abstract. As a famous statistician once said, "All models are wrong, but some are useful." This means that even the most rigorous analysis will fail to fully describe reality and therefore will require some translation to actual situations. At the same time, scientific rigor is needed to root the interpretation in truth. The most effective assessments are simultaneously credible and compelling.

Credibility is established through a foundation in data and scientific methods. Demonstrating that you have considered all elements and taken steps to reduce bias or measurement error establishes credibility in the results drawn from the assessment. To be compelling, the assessment needs to read like a relatable story that is grounded in real experiences and considers practical constraints. Whether the story retells a real situation or explores realistic hypotheticals, it needs to synthesize all the scientific information and integrate it with real-world aspects. The artfulness of the process shines through here most vividly.

In the CLABSI example, the technical results are the changes in the rates of CLABSIs, while the practical realities involve the barriers to implementation and the solutions that were identified. When the insurance company communicates, the results of their assessment to current prospective members, the data and research supporting the claims of the benefits of mental and behavioral health services provide credibility. Interpreting the impact of these services on individual lives and providing details regarding how we would access and receive the services contribute to a compelling story the intended audience can picture themselves being part of.

8.5.1.4 Identify Learnings and New Insights

Principle #4: Value assessments may demonstrate what you know to be true, but they may also identify what you didn't know. In addition to informing or persuading, you can use a value assessment to explore. We're often reluctant to proceed with an analysis or assessment without knowing (or at least being confident of) the outcome in advance. We shouldn't be. Instead of fearing uncertainty, we should embrace the knowledge that we will likely learn something new even if it's not what we had hoped. If done well, a value assessment reveals something new or even unexpected that will better equip us to understand how best to proceed.

Quality and value are linked; quality and financial return may not be. That means that comprehensive, effective, patient-centered care is likely to be extremely valuable in the broader sense. But it may be financially unfeasible to provide or sustain, implying only that you've yet to figure out how to align the financial incentives with the overall value produced by the care solution.

A thorough examination of the sources and magnitudes of the costs and benefits may reveal which components are critical for financial viability. Maybe it's about volume; maybe it's about efficient application to the right patient population; maybe it's about leveraging technology in the right way; or maybe it's something else completely.

In developing the value assessment of the CLABSI initiative, it is possible that potentially valuable spillover effects were excluded from the calculations because they were not even considered when the initiative was being developed. Perhaps only when the initiative started and the assessment was being performed did it become clear that likely ancillary benefits of the initiative existed for reducing other types of infections or safety-related events. It may have required performing the assessment to truly understand the extent to which spillover effects can occur. In the insurance company example, perhaps while performing the value assessment the company realized that members may actually incur costs of remaining members that were unknowable, such as forgoing any savings they may have experienced by switching to their spouse's plan.

8.5.1.5   Describe What's Needed Going Forward

Principle #5: Value assessments should not be a one-time endeavor. All useful healthcare-related metrics should be repeatedly evaluated, including metrics of value. To truly understand the value associated with a process, product, device, or solution, we need to assess the value at multiple time points and monitor key metrics. Circumstances change, policies are revised, unforeseen crises consume the attention of healthcare workers, and clinical knowledge evolves. Repeated assessments or ongoing monitoring may be prudent depending on the situation.

Those who performed the assessment of the CLABSI initiative suggest that future evaluations of the sustainability of the initiative will be performed and the financial return to the hospital will be updated at that time. For the insurance company, they claim to have the intention to evaluate changes in mental and behavioral health service use and estimate potential value realized by members who utilized those services.

8.6   Summary

The value assessment framework presented in this chapter can serve as a guide for those designing, developing, and performing value assessments. Within the three main components of (1) defining value, (2) identifying costs, benefits, and metrics, and (3) interpreting and communicating results, several key subcomponents will help clarify and solidify a good assessment. Within each of these three components, specifying certain details will help clarify and focus the assessment. For example, identifying the perspective, scope, and intended audience will often illuminate which costs and benefits are relevant; determining the goal or motivation of the assessment may determine which metrics are the most appropriate for communicating the key message. When leveraged, the value framework will allow for more structured assessments and provide audiences with the necessary information to evaluate the results. Additionally, assessments developed with this framework may be more easily compared and contrasted.

Reference

1. Solid CA (2020) Return on investment for healthcare quality improvement. Springer Nature, Cham

Chapter 9
Examples and Practical Suggestions

9.1 Real-World Examples

The previous chapter explored examples based on real situations and common initiatives, but the examples were hypothetical. While using hypothetical examples allows us to tailor characteristics of the examples to clearly illustrate key points, real situations are often more complicated and nuanced. Therefore, we will explore how we could apply the value assessment framework to real-world programs or initiatives to see how it handles complication and nuance.

I do not attempt to fully quantify or calculate value in these examples; instead I seek to illustrate how we could apply the value assessment framework in order to perform a full assessment.

9.1.1 Example 1: Determining Value Within the CMS Hospital Readmissions Reduction Program

It may be dangerous to wander into these woods because of the political and financial implications surrounding federal quality monitoring programs, but given the immense weight our health system is putting on value-based reimbursement programs and the fact that CMS is the largest purveyor of such systems, it seems necessary to explore a CMS-funded value-based program. Please note that this is not an attempt to render a verdict on the worth of the program or to suggest future policy. Instead, the goal is to illustrate how we could use the framework proposed in the previous chapter to evaluate this type of program or use it to design a similar program.

As we walk through this example, you may discover that depending on how it is defined, measured, and communicated, the value expressed from the program fluctuates considerably. This is not uncommon, and it is exactly why a framework is

© The Author(s), under exclusive license to Springer Nature Switzerland AG 2022
C. A. Solid, *Practical Strategies to Assess Value in Health Care*,
https://doi.org/10.1007/978-3-030-95149-8_9

critical: Value without structure reverts to the subjective concept we started with; applying a framework allows for specific evaluation and meaningful comparisons.

For those not familiar with the CMS Hospital Readmission Reduction Program, it was initiated in 2010 with a goal to reduce 30-day rehospitalization rates among fee-for-service US hospitals. The program calculates 30-day risk-adjusted readmission rates for six conditions (acute myocardial infarction, chronic obstructive pulmonary disease, congestive heart failure, pneumonia, coronary artery bypass graft surgery, and elective hip or knee arthroplasty). Participating hospitals face the possibility of receiving bonuses or penalties equal to 3% of their overall reimbursement for a particular condition [1], depending on their performance on the rehospitalization rate compared with their peers.

Since its inception, there has been no shortage of studies and articles challenging the merits and specifications of the program. Some authors have taken issue with how hospitalizations are defined, and others bemoan the adequacy of the risk adjustment methods or limitations in coding systems to accurately reflect the conditions studied. Some have claimed that the program may unintentionally penalize those serving high-risk patients.

Some studies have also examined aspects of hospitalizations and rehospitalizations that those who framed the details of the program may have never considered. One such study endeavored to determine whether hospitals with a greater share of Medicare-covered patients might be incentivized to pursue more improvement in the Medicare-based program; another hypothesized that having a hospital-based skilled nursing facility for post-acute care would be associated with lower readmission rates. The list goes on. The point is that in each case, authors have sought to explore or evaluate some component of quality, fairness, or effectiveness, presumably to assess the value associated with the program. Each has a valid point, but each uses a different definition for value and different methods and metrics to perform their assessment.

Let us consider how we might use the framework (Table 9.1) to perform a specific assessment of the value of this program, starting from a payer point of view.

Step 1: Define value. From a payer **perspective**, value would likely be defined by utilization or in monetary terms; for example, the total cost avoidance from reductions in 30-day readmission. Depending on the goal or decision to be informed, the **scope** may include all patients and conditions, or it might include a subset of one or both. Regardless, the specific scope will carry with it specific **assumptions**, such as what will be considered a readmission and how rates are calculated (using risk adjustment, etc.) and how much of any observed reduction in rates will be attributed directly to the program. Given the perspective taken, perhaps the most appropriate **audience** would be policy makers, so that the **goal** is to demonstrate that the program was "worth it" from a fiscal standpoint.

When value is defined using all five components in the framework (perspective, scope, assumptions, audience, and goal), we can immediately see what is relevant and what is extraneous and will already form expectations regarding what will be included in the costs and benefits used to establish value. Unintended consequences related to condition-specific outcomes or administrative burden of individual

Table 9.1 The value assessment framework

Framework component	Description
Define value	
Perspective	Value to whom?
Scope	Specify details related to the timing, setting, intensity, population, and duration the assessment covers
Goal(s) or objective(s)	Clearly state the motivation, goals, purpose, or the decision the assessment will inform
Assumptions	Identify the assumptions used in the value assessment and explicitly state them
Intended audience	Determine for whom you are performing the assessment
Identify costs, benefits, and metrics	
Cost sources and measurements	Identify the sources of the costs and benefits, determine the measurements and quantification of each cost and benefit, and establish the level of attribution they have to the intervention, product, service, or solution being assessed
Benefit sources and measurements	
Appropriate metrics	Explore various metrics that may be useful; there may be multiple metrics appropriate for the same assessment. Identify relevant comparisons or benchmarks if applicable
Interpret and communicate	
Explore all types of value	Value is more than financial return; be sure to explore nonmonetary costs and benefits and place the results in context
Inform, guide, and teach	A value assessment should do more than just restate what we already know
Merge practical and technical considerations	Combining technical results with practical realities can help make the assessment credible and compelling
Identify learnings and new insights	Describe anything new or previously unknown that the value assessment unearthed
Describe what's needed going forward	Value assessments should not be a one-time endeavor

hospitals, unless they directly impact the cost savings realized by CMS, will not be considered. That does not mean that they have no value. It simply reflects that they lie outside the strict definition of value in this case. Whether you agree or disagree with that definition is a separate point—at least you are clear about what the definition entails and how it will be used.

Step 2: Determine costs, benefits, and metrics. Given value definition (specifically the scope and perspective), the **costs** are likely to be the administrative and oversight cost incurred by CMS (either directly or through payments to organizations that have contracts to serve as the administrators). The **benefits** reflect the monetary savings from no longer having to pay for hospitalizations that would have occurred after risk adjusting and accounting for the stated level of attribution (i.e., how much of the observed reduction is attributed to the program). **Metrics** may be ROI, total cost savings, the number of hospitalizations avoided, or other aggregated measures. More than likely, **reasonable comparisons** would be the monetary cost of the program (that is, achieving an ROI greater than 0%) or the monetary return that may have been realized by an alternative program that could have received the funding.

If the determination of costs, benefits, and metrics seems straightforward, it should. What constitutes relevant costs and benefits and what types of metrics and benchmarks are useful will typically follow directly from a clear definition of value. We are not left wondering whether patient experience is a benefit—while it may be in a general sense, it is not considered as part of this assessment because of the perspective we have chosen. While the costs and benefits may not be inclusive of all the realized costs and benefits of all stakeholders, they clearly signal what type of interpretation may be reasonable.

Step 3: Interpret and communicate. It may be that the financial return reflects most of the value for this assessment, at least the way it is set up. However, if the return was small or even negative, in evaluating the merits of the program we may **consider other types of value**, including nonmonetary and/or societal benefits not captured by the given metrics. Ideally, the interpretation of this type of assessment would acknowledge and even welcome the critiques offered by other authors regarding the methods of risk adjustment or introduction of unintended consequences. In this way, the assessment could **inform, guide, and teach** how to improve certain methods for future iterations and consider **practical realities** regarding the administration of the program or the reasonableness of attributing changes in readmission directly to the efforts of the program. **Future** iterations of the assessment could then examine how any alterations to the program specifications impacted the value as defined.

As described, the results of the assessment are multifaceted. They likely will inform decisions regarding future investments into this or similar programs, but they also speak to the components of the program that may have affected the value as defined. Other assessments that seek to examine the impact of risk adjustment, patient case mix, the presence of skilled nursing facilities, or other factors, may define and measure value differently; but if they are clearly specified, we can more easily compare and combine them to create a full picture of the value of the program.

Consider an alternative assessment of the CMS Hospital Readmission Reduction Program that takes a patient perspective and considers benefits as measured by simply the number of hospitalizations avoided versus the costs of potential unintended consequences related to care and the patient experience. Perhaps in such an assessment, a relevant benchmark or comparison would be other activities patients could engage in to avoid rehospitalizations, such as hiring an in-home care provider or opting for long-term post-acute care. The point is that value is defined very differently, with different metrics and comparisons for what constitutes "good" or "better." There is not necessarily a right or a wrong type of assessment; each has use for some decision maker(s), even if the results of the different assessments are not directly comparable.

A key takeaway from the hospital readmission example should be that when specific parameters regarding a value definition (such as the perspective, goal, and intended audience in the previous above) are lacking, the program opens itself to wide-ranging criticism because of the numerous ways we could consider components of value. Leaving the definition of value (and the purpose behind that definition) unspecified or broad invites reproach from various directions where evaluators choose to consider different perspectives, metrics, or motivations to determine the value of this and other programs. Requiring yourself to specify each component will inevitably narrow the applicability or generalizability, but the increased focus and direction will force you to think more critically about all parts of the analysis and ultimately will produce results that are more easily leveraged to make your point or influence your audience.

9.1.2   Example 2: Determining the Value of a Medical Device or Digital Health Application

In the spirit of offering perhaps a more readily usable example, we will walk through how a medical device company would endeavor to demonstrate the value of their device first to a payer (in an attempt to secure contracts or be covered by that payer) and second to another organization (in an attempt to be acquired by that organization). This example clearly resides within the realm of "making the business case" in the more traditional sense and will inherently involve fewer theoretical concepts and more practical ones. Hopefully, the juxtaposition with the previous example will help you better understand how we can apply the framework to different situations.

A quick search of a publicly available database[1] reveals that as of this writing, 63 for-profit companies in the United States have a device, system, app, process, or platform whose sole purpose is to help patients be more adherent to their medications. Among those that have received funding (approximately half of the 63 mentioned), the total amount of funding reported in this database ranges from a paltry $20,000 to an impressive $49 million; a handful of the companies have acquired other companies or been acquired themselves.

Given these figures, it follows that improving medication adherence must hold significant value for one or more perspectives. That can really be the only explanation for why dozens of companies pursuing various innovations have been launched and why investors are willing to invest tens of millions of dollars in some of them. Therefore, it may be reasonable for one of these companies to believe that their proprietary "adherence solution" may be attractive to a payer or potentially acquiring organization.

Let's explore how one of these med-tech companies may construct a value assessment to present to these audiences to illustrate how they could apply the framework.

---

[1] Crunchbase.com

9.1.2.1 The Value Assessment for a Payer Audience

To start, let's consider how this may look if the med-tech company is trying to convince a payer of the value of their solution.

Step 1: Define Value. In their value assessment, the med-tech company would want to take the payer's **perspective**, which means that they will need to focus on financial costs and benefits to and for the payer, including the potential cost savings from less utilization for treating adverse events that are associated with poor medication adherence. The **goal** may be obvious: To convince the payer (the **audience**) that the improvement in adherence will more than pay for the cost of the med-tech's solution through fewer adverse events that require costly health encounters. Identifying the **scope** for this assessment will likely involve careful consideration of several factors in order to ensure they can demonstrate significant value for the payer. For example, they may first consider the payer's member makeup. If the payer is an employer group health plan covering working-age and healthier members, the need among members for assistance with medication management may be less than for a Medicare Advantage plan that covers older adults who may be more likely to have more complex medication regimens. Second, the med-tech company will want to carefully consider what data and information are available to make their case before they decide on their scope. For example, perhaps extensive data demonstrate poor adherence among a specific patient group (e.g., those with a particular disease burden, like diabetes and hypertension, where the risks of poor adherence are serious and expensive) or that the company's own research has shown that their solution is especially effective for certain types of individuals (e.g., those taking five or more medications who are living alone). Basically, the med-tech company will want to think through the potential opportunity for capturing value for a specific scope and/or patient population.[2] Often, this is a major challenge for med-tech and device companies: Getting clear about the targeted population and balancing the desire for their solution to apply to as many people as possible realizing that it will likely produce a higher financial return among certain individuals.

As part of the determination of scope, the med-tech company will consider the **assumptions** necessary to estimate the value for that scope. That is, they will probably not have access to the payer's actual patient population and will have to assume a certain number of affected members. Then, they will need to make certain assumptions regarding things like:

- The current level of medication adherence
- The increased risk of adverse events as a result of poor adherence
- Payer-incurred costs to treat those adverse events
- The extent to which the med-tech company's solution can improve adherence and reduce the risk of adverse events to save payer costs

---

[2] If this sounds like the process I described in Chap. 8, it is because identifying the potential opportunity and impact is often a crucial step; details in that section can illustrate this more fully.

The last point may require additional assumptions, such as why patients are non-adherent, to justify why they believe their solution will improve adherence. For example, if the med-tech's solution involves reminders and/or special packaging to help individuals take the correct doses of the correct medications at the correct times, the ability of that to impact adherence assumes that currently, forgetfulness or confusion is contributing to poor adherence. If an individual was not taking their medication simply because he or she did not believe it was effective, this med-tech's solution may not impact that person's adherence.

Step 2: Determine Costs, Benefits, and Metrics. You can already see that compared with the previous example, this value assessment requires much more effort and thought to define value. However, clearly defining value in the first step makes it easier to determine the relevant costs and benefits, as well as which metrics will be appropriate to achieve the med-tech company's stated goal. The **costs** from the payer's perspective will be the cost of the med-tech company's solution. The magnitude of the costs will be related to the scope chosen previously. The more patients the med-tech company proposes it would benefit, the higher the costs. The **benefits** will be the cost avoidance the payer experiences from less care utilization stemming from fewer adverse events that occur when an individual's medication adherence improves. This will be the crux of the value proposition for the med-tech company and will depend on several of the bulleted assumptions listed in the Value Definition section of this example. Given that this example considers only financial costs and benefits, the appropriate **metrics** will likely be ROI, total cost savings, savings per patient, or similar metrics.

Step 3: Interpret and Communicate Results. This example is common in that the entire quantification of value is financial. However, for the interpretation and presentation to the payer, this med-tech company would still want to discuss **nonfinancial components of value**. This may involve discussing how assisting with medication adherence can also improve their members' overall well-being and quality of life, potential impacts on member satisfaction, and maybe even member retention. This helps place the quantified financial value in context and suggest it as only part of the overall value the med-tech company's solution contributes.

Depending on the chosen scope, the opportunity to **inform, guide, and teach** may take the form of quantifying the current risk exposure the payer faces. That is, calculating the total cost the payer may be incurring solely due to poor medication adherence may serve to highlight the potential opportunity to improve care even if the payer was already generally aware of the negative impacts of poor adherence. While the data used to estimate the potential cost savings reflects **technical considerations**, the med-tech company can demonstrate their knowledge of real-world components of care by discussing the **practical considerations** related to how patients will access the solution (i.e., if it is a device, it will need to be distributed; if it is an app or a platform, it will need to be downloaded or accessed) and any training that will be necessary. If the med-tech company's solution contains an electronic tracking component, it may be possible for the payer to perform **ongoing assessments** of improvements in adherence and track associated reductions in adverse events and spending.

Define Value	Identify Costs, Benefits, Metrics	Interpret and Communicate
Scope: chronic disease patients on 3+ medications	Costs: cost of the device	All types of value: Patient well-being, satisfaction, retention
Perspective: the payer	Benefits: cost avoidance from fewer adverse events	Inform, guide, teach: quantification of the current risk exposure from adherence
Goal: convince the payer to pay for the device	Metrics: ROI, total cost savings, savings per patient	Practical + technical: how patients will access the solution, necessary training
Audience: the payer		New insights: the magnitude of the costs associated with adherence
Assumptions: current adherence and associated costs, impact of device, etc.		Going forward: tracking improvements in adherence and related cost reductions

Fig. 9.1 The value assessment framework for the medical device example: A payer organization as the audience

A visual representation of the framework in this case is shown in Fig. 9.1. Displaying it this way will be helpful when examining what would change if we performed the value assessment for a different audience and goal.

If the med-tech company can create a credible and compelling case for the value for the payer, they will likely increase their chances of securing a contract to supply their solution. In the discourse between med-tech company and payer, there may be a number of iterations in the value assessment as the payer poses questions or reacts to the assumptions presented by the med-tech company. Having a framework that clearly lays out the components will help direct those conversations and may illustrate to the payer the thoroughness of the med-tech company's preparation. Situations occur where payers and those proposing a specific solution can almost work together to construct the business case. However, this typically only occurs when the assessment is well thought out and organized.

9.1.2.2   The Value Assessment for a Potentially Acquiring Organization

It is instructive to consider how an assessment of value for the same medical device used in the last example would change simply by changing the intended audience from a payer to an organization that would consider acquiring the company.

First, the **definition of value** will likely be similar but may include some additional components. The similarities will stem from the fact that whoever owns the proprietary technology or details of the solution for improving adherence, the value of that solution to those who pay for care will remain. Additional components may

Define Value	**Identify Costs, Benefits, Metrics**	**Interpret and Communicate**
Scope: chronic disease patients on 3+ medications	Costs: cost of the **acquisition**	All types of value: **market capture, growth potential, etc.**
Perspective: the payer **and acquiring organization**	Benefits: cost avoidance from fewer adverse events, **additional revenues**	Inform, guide, teach: **the size of the potential market, revenue opportunity**
Goal: convince the **organization to acquire the device company**	Metrics: ROI, total cost savings, savings per patient, **market share, customer base increases, etc.**	Practical + technical: how patients will access the solution, necessary training
Audience: the **potentially acquiring organization**		New insights: the magnitude of the costs associated with adherence
Assumptions: current adherence and associated costs, impact of device, etc.		Going forward: **projections of future value and plan to monitor value in the future**

Fig. 9.2 The value assessment framework for the medical device example: A potentially acquiring organization as the audience

come from additional market capture the solution provides or from any complementary services or products the acquiring organization already has. For example, perhaps the acquiring organization has a telehealth product and the med-tech's solution is an app or web-based platform that can easily be incorporated into the acquiring organization's current technology. Then, the med-tech company may want to define value so that it includes the potential cost savings to the acquiring organization of not having to develop an adherence solution from scratch, or the potential increase in clientele that may be attracted by the addition of the adherence solution.

The relevant **costs and benefits**, as well as the appropriate **metrics**, would be similarly adjusted. That is, costs would include more than just the price of the solution itself (assuming the acquiring organization would buy out the technology and absorb the current med-tech company), and the benefits would incorporate estimates related to the increased market capture and potential revenue increases from the additional service offering of assisting with adherence.

Clearly, the **interpretation and communication** of the results would also change. It is likely that much of the illustration of potential savings from the payer perspective would remain, but there would also be an illustration of the "business case" as it relates to market share, customer base, and any impact the device may have on complementary devices the acquiring organization already offers. Figure 9.2 illustrates how the components of the value assessment framework could change when the audience changes to a potentially acquiring organization. Differences or additions from Fig. 9.1 are in bold type.

9.1.3   Example 3: Determining the Value of Primary Care

The previous two examples represent targeted interventions and consider primarily financial value. Could we apply the value assessment framework to a larger but less specific area of care? Could the framework help answer, for example, a question like, "What is the value of primary care?" Let us examine how that would work.

To begin, we should acknowledge the documented challenges primary care physicians and practices face and explore the current discussions regarding the contribution of and payment structures for primary care services. In 2021, the National Academies of Sciences, Engineering, and Medicine released a consensus study report that summarizes many of these challenges and suggests steps for implementing change [2]. This 400-plus page report cites data indicating that primary care accounts for 35% of healthcare visits but receives only about 5% of healthcare expenditures. Additionally, the number of primary care providers is shrinking as more clinicians are choosing to specialize in fields that offer higher monetary compensation. Extensive research by dozens of institutions and authors has repeatedly shown that primary care is associated with improved access to care services, better patient outcomes and population health measures (including mortality, infant birth weight, life expectancy), and less use of high-cost utilization like hospitalization and ED visits [3, 4].

Primary care is also associated with more equitable population health and can have a significantly positive impact on health status for racial and ethnic minorities and those of low socioeconomic status. Its benefits stem from the services it offers: general wellness care (education, preventive services, etc.), the identification and management of chronic conditions, serving as a first contact for patients when health issues arise to either treat or refer to a specialist, and the reduction in unnecessary or inappropriate specialty care [4, 5].

The available research illustrates the myriad of ways primary care provides value to patients. A partial list includes:

- Disease prevention (which can reduce disease burden of illnesses through activities like vaccination)
- Earlier disease detection (through cancer screenings, etc.)
- Chronic care management
- Treatment of nonemergency injuries
- Increased access to care
- Population health equality
- Lower mortality
- Higher infant birth weights
- Longer life expectancy
- Fewer hospitalizations and ED visits
- Greater weight loss among obese individuals
- Having a trusted medical professional to ask questions of

While such an extensive list suggests that significant value exists, it can also pose a challenge for a value assessment seeking to demonstrate or quantify that value, given the volume and variety of the potential value sources. In many ways, having a standard framework is even more crucial for a situation like this than for assessments of individual or short-term interventions. A value assessment of primary care could be designed and executed any number of ways; what follows is not a suggestion of how it should be done but simply an illustration of how the proposed framework can help guide the assessment's development. We will assume that a group that advocates for the primary care industry is performing the assessment and that their ultimate goal is to encourage policy changes that will improve primary care payments to be in line with what the group feels is warranted. The group wants the assessment to be appropriate for an audience of policy makers but also for the general public to garner support among voters to help encourage policy makers to take action.

   Step 1: Define Value. Given the stated **goal** and intended **audiences**, it is reasonable to assume that the assessment would be performed from the **patient perspective**. The **scope** of this type of assessment is broad, but could legitimately be defined as "all primary care" or "all forms of care delivered by primary care teams." When seeking a comprehensive definition of value, as in this case, some of the **assumptions** may be relevant when the individual benefit sources are identified. For example, while most agree that preventive health can help avoid or reduce the severity of certain conditions, the assessment would need to assume a certain level of impact on the subsequent incidence of conditions that could be directly attributed to the existence of primary care. However, for this step, it may be enough to define value in general terms so that the value of primary care represents "patient benefits through increased health, reduced care utilization and expenditure, and overall well-being and satisfaction with the healthcare system," as an example. Details of specific benefit sources could follow in the next step.

   Step 2: Determine Costs, Benefits, and Metrics. Given the goal of this assessment, those involved in its development could choose to address **costs** a number of ways. The easiest would be to avoid them altogether so that the assessment simply attempts to quantify the benefits of primary care to inform what would be a reasonable level of investment in primary care. A more complete assessment, however, would involve current payments and investments in infrastructure to support primary care to allow for the comparison to benefits and interpret the results to make the case for why higher spending is warranted. As stated previously, enumerating **benefits** would be prudent given the extensiveness of their type and variety. It may also be that the degree to which the benefits can be reliably measured and/or quantified will vary across identified benefits, too. This can make it difficult to aggregate the individual sources into one or a handful of overall **metrics**. Assessors will need to determine whether to construct multiple metrics that are appropriate for the individual benefits (perhaps aggregating some that are similar, such as all the financial benefits) and how best to summarize the total value to best communicate their message. Regarding relevant **comparisons**, the assessment could choose to discuss the benefits in light of the magnitude of benefits of specialties or in comparison to national metrics (e.g., GDP, benefits from social services like Social Security) as a way to give weight to the quantities calculated.

Step 3: Interpret and Communicate Results. There is no doubt that an effective message about the value of primary care would incorporate **both financial and other types of value**. While patients and policy makers are interested in out-of-pocket healthcare spending, they are also very interested in general well-being, quality of life, and population health. An assessment would seek to **inform, guide, and teach** the general public about the importance of primary care and discrepancies in the size of its role compared to the funding it receives. By merging **technical research** about the benefits associated with primary care with **practical considerations** related to access to care and social determinants, the assessment can also encourage action **going forward**, presumably by encouraging policy makers to act and advocating for a particular reimbursement mechanism or system.

Hopefully, these examples serve to illustrate how the value assessment framework can be applied to a variety of situations. In each case, a real assessment would include much more detail and have specifics, where in some instances I left broad statements. These examples are not intended to be precise templates, nor are they meant to suggest a correct or incorrect way to apply the recommendations contained throughout this book. Through your own experiences and understanding of the unique initiatives, products, devices, or processes you wish to evaluate, you will likely develop your own templates or best practices for how to develop and carry out value assessments. I hope that what I have presented so far provides you with a place to start and a foundation from which to build upon.

As a final offering, I put forward some thoughts and practical suggestions that may give you additional assistance and guidance.

9.2 General Thoughts and Practical Suggestions for Developing and Carrying Out Value Assessments

As mentioned previously, you will develop your own specific strategies and regular practices as you gain experience with developing and carrying out value assessments. However, I offer some of my own learnings in the hope that they may either help or spark ideas of tips that will be more relevant for your unique situation.

9.2.1 Collect and Organize Relevant Information

The concept of value encompasses a great many things in health care. Therefore, there is no shortage of information sources that may be relevant to one type of value assessment or another. If you believe you will ever attempt to assess value, have a location (physical or electronic) where you can start collecting articles, books, links, thoughts, notes, and data that speak to value in some way, shape, or form. Even if it remains unorganized, such a collection can save countless hours when developing value assessments by simply serving as a central repository for all things value related. Relevant information to collect could include:

- Data on disease incidence and prevalence for a particular clinical area
- Estimates or data on monetary costs of treatments, health events, or care delivery activities
- Effectiveness of interventions, initiatives, and/or devices on specific disease states or the risks of adverse events
- Explorations of (and even personal narratives about) quality of life, patient experiences, and the components of health and health care that affect them
- Reports on relevant health policy changes and general trends in disease, mortality, reimbursement, and relevant costs and benefits
- Previous examples of value assessments, both for the information they contain on costs and benefits, but also as examples or templates to use

If and when you decide to apply some level of organization to the information you collect, consider whether it makes the most sense to organize it by clinical topic, type of value (e.g., monetary, quality of life, efficiency, etc.), or perspective. This will be a function of the information but also of your needs, preferences, and usual practices. For example, if you exclusively perform value assessments from a payer perspective, organizing by perspective may not serve you well.

9.2.2   Develop and Use Templates

Having a system or template can drastically reduce the time you spend developing value assessments and can help eliminate the likelihood that you will forget something or fail to consider an important component. Here I offer a few examples that may be helpful or will provide a starting point for the development of your own templates. The first is the value assessment framework—an expansion of the value framework into a worksheet with room to write notes or specific details for each component (Fig. 9.3).

In some instances, it can be helpful to have templates that are specific for individual components that are often challenging. One that I have used with clients appears as Table 9.2. In the left-hand column appear the most common (but not all) benefit sources as described in Chap. 8, and across the columns to the right are different perspectives that might be relevant. Within the cells, you can add notes for specific information or simply add a check for those that apply. I have added entries based on the CLABSI example from the previous chapter to illustrate how a completed table might look.

Instead of simply checking which benefits may be relevant for which perspectives, you could also add notes regarding what the benefit is, how it is measured, and so on. When I employ this tool, clients often discover multiple benefit sources they

Framework Component	Notes
Define Value	
Perspective	
Scope	
Goal(s) or Objective(s)	
Assumptions	
Intended Audience	
Identify Costs, Benefits, and Metrics	
Cost Sources and Measurements	
Benefit Sources and Measurements	
Appropriate Metrics	
Interpret and Communicate	
Explore all Types of Value	
Inform, Guide, and Teach	
Merge Practical and Technical Considerations	
Identify Learnings and New Insights	
Describe What's Needed Going Forward	

Fig. 9.3 Value assessment framework worksheet

have not previously considered. Obviously, this could be adjusted to include different perspectives or additional value sources since the list in the left-hand column is not exhaustive or even inclusive of everything mentioned about the five benefits explained in Chap. 8.

I have also developed a shorter tool specifically designed for device or med-tech companies that hope to demonstrate the value of their product to a payer like a health plan or insurance company. An image of it follows and can serve to assist device and med-tech companies when determining how to formulate or consider their value proposition (Fig. 9.4).

Table 9.2 Checklist of most common sources of benefits

Source	Patients	Payer	Provider	Societal
Utilization				
Lower incidence or prevalence of disease				
Fewer adverse events	✓	✓		
Lower intensity or length of care	✓		✓	
Efficiency				
Lower resource use				
Fewer errors		✓	✓	
More continuous care				
Patient experience or health				
Improved quality of life	✓			
Higher satisfaction with care	✓			
Reduced disease burden	✓			
Improved emotional well-being	✓			
Administrative				
Increased revenue from risk pools			✓	
Patient/member retention			✓	
Improved brand or reputation			✓	
Societal				
Increased work productivity				
Improved equity				
Improved access to care				

As with the other templates, you can alter this for your purposes and add detail, but it may serve as a foundation to build upon.

9.2.3   How to Standardize Value Assessment Results

In early chapters of this book, I have discussed how the lack of consistency in the definition of value or in how assessments of value are designed or performed has made it difficult to make meaningful comparisons across initiatives, care settings, or even years. It seems prudent then to explore how we could use the value assessment framework to introduce some standardization into value assessments in order to allow for direct comparisons.

The manner in which this would be accomplished depends on the situation and the type of comparisons you hope to make. Types of standardizations could involve:

- The value definition (e.g., a standard time frame, patient population, or setting)
- The assumptions (e.g., a standard value for the cost avoidance of a specific event, the level of attribution for a particular type of intervention)

To Demonstrate the Value of Your Device to a Payer:

Show that there is a need or an opportunity for improvement	+	Show the magnitude of your solution's impact on that opportunity

Size of Opportunity

Care Pathway

What's true about the issue your solution targets?

☐ It relates to a common condition or event

☐ Care or treatment is frequent and/or costly

☐ It is important to patients and/or their families

☐ The solutions currently available fail to fully address the issue(s)

Magnitude of Impact

Which of these does the solution accomplish?

☐ Reduces the risk of adverse events

☐ Improves patient outcomes

☐ Impacts most or all of the target population

☐ Improves disease management or patient behavior (better medication adherence, lifestyle choices, etc.)

☐ Increases the efficiency of care (reduces waste)

Practical Considerations
Which of the following apply?

Measurement	**Feasibility**	**Timing of benefit(s)**
☐ It is quantifiable	There is evidence that:	☐ Within 1st 12 months
☐ It is monetizable	☐ Patients will use it	☐ Long term
☐ There are data available	☐ Clinicians will use it	☐ On-going

Appropriate method for demonstrating value:	☐ Literature Summary	☐ Data analysis or pilot study	☐ ROI analysis

Fig. 9.4 Quick tool for medical device and med-tech companies wanting to demonstrate value to a payer

- The costs or benefits (e.g., a standard source or method for measuring or quantifying either a cost or benefit, a standard conversation to use when estimating the financial value of a particular type of nonmonetary cost or benefit)
- The metrics used (e.g., ROI, cost per unit benefit)

And there may be others, depending on the goals or desired comparisons. For example, if CMS wished to compare the value of different quality improvement initiatives or quality monitoring programs, then several things could be implemented to increase standardization. For initiatives or programs evaluating the rate of specific events, such as hospitalizations or infections, CMS could impose a standard value for the cost avoidance of each type of event and use the same data source to quantify or estimate the number of events avoided. That way, different initiatives that attempt to reduce the adverse event through different methods could use many of the same quantities to calculate value.

Alternatively, CMS could also establish a set of standard metrics that each initiative should calculate. For example, again using adverse event avoidance, if each initiative included as one of its metrics the cost per event avoided, CMS could do the following: It could quickly look to see which initiative attempted to reduce, say, hospitalizations and cost the least per hospitalization avoided, even without applying a standardized cost avoidance value per hospitalization.

A hospital that wants to standardize value assessment results may establish a set of common assumptions or estimates across the facility so that each department uses the same basis for calculating metrics. This also would allow more direct comparisons over time (if appropriately discounted) to more accurately track progress.

It is difficult to know what types of standardization would be most appropriate for a given situation, but hopefully encouraging organizations to consider it and providing a framework to work from will produce value assessments that can more readily be compared.

References

1. Centers for Medicare & Medicaid Services (CMS) (2021) Hospital Readmissions Reduction Program (HRRP). https://www.cms.gov/Medicare/Medicare-Fee-for-Service-Payment/AcuteInpatientPPS/Readmissions-Reduction-Program. Accessed 31 Aug 2021
2. National Academies of Sciences Engineering and Medicine (2021) Implementing high-quality primary care: rebuilding the Foundation of Health Care. The National Academies Press, Washington, DC. https://doi.org/10.17226/25983
3. Shi L (2012) The impact of primary care: a focused review. Scientifica 2012:432892. https://doi.org/10.6064/2012/432892
4. Starfield B, Shi L, Macinko J (2005) Contribution of primary care to health systems and health. Milbank Q 83(3):457–502. https://doi.org/10.1111/j.1468-0009.2005.00409.x
5. Miller HD (2021) Patient-centered payment for primary care. Center for Healthcare Quality & Payment Reform

Glossary of Terms

ACA Affordable Care Act of 2010.

APM Alternative payment model: one of the value-based payment model options available for those who treat Medicare patients.

BCR Benefit-to-cost ratio: an alternative or supplement to ROI, and is calculated as the benefits divided by the costs; can be interpreted as "the benefits per dollar spent".

Benchmark A value by which to compare and evaluate results or outcomes.

Care Delivery Systems Any organized group that attempts to provide care to individuals; examples include hospitals, clinics, emergency departments, and health systems.

CBO Community-based organization: an organization outside of traditional healthcare delivery systems that provides support services that may assist community-dwelling individuals to maintain health.

CEA Cost-effectiveness analysis: an economic method to establish the financial justification for a particular activity.

CLABSI Central line-associated bloodstream infections: a common quality measure that tracks the rate of this infection in healthcare settings.

CMS The Centers for Medicare and Medicaid Services.

Complex Adaptive Systems A type of system made up of independent but semiautonomous individuals who interact with each other in multiple ways.

CUA Cost–utility analysis: an economic method to establish the cost per quality-adjusted life years that a change in policy or activities would yield.

Discount Rate The annual percentage rate used to calculate the present value of future costs or benefits.

ED Emergency department.

FFS Fee-for-service: a health reimbursement policy by which providers and facilities are paid based on the services they provide, regardless of patient outcomes.

ICER Incremental cost-effectiveness ratio: a ratio of the difference in cost to the difference in QALYs in a cost-effectiveness or cost–utility analysis.

ICU Intensive care unit.

Implementation Science A field that endeavors to understand how innovations or changes are best implemented and sustained in healthcare delivery systems.

MACRA The Medicare Access and CHIP Reauthorization Act of 2015, which mandated the creation of an incentive program for providers where reimbursement was in part based on performance on quality measures.

Moral Hazard The tendency to either engage in more risky behavior or consume more healthcare services because of the presence of health insurance.

Net Benefits Benefits minus costs.

Payback Period The time until costs are covered by accumulating benefits.

Perspective The selected point of view for a given ROI analysis.

Population Health The health status and outcomes of a group of people instead of that of an individual.

QALY Quality-adjusted life years: a calculation of the total survival time adjusted to reflect the quality of life during that time.

Reliability An indication of how well a quality measure can detect differences in quality between entities.

ROI Return on investment.

Savings Per Patient Net benefits per patient affected.

Scope The selected time frame and affected population for an ROI analysis.

TPHO Third-party healthcare organization: a perspective that includes device, med-tech, and pharmaceutical companies and community services, including community-based organizations.

Validity An indication of how well a quality measure reflects the concept it is attempting to measure.

Index